296.74
K31   Kemelman, Haim.
           How to live in the
present tense.

DATE	ISSUED TO
NO 15 '71	

296.74
K31   Kemelman, Haim.
           How to live in the
present tense.

Temple Israel Library
Minneapolis, Minn.

Please sign your full name on the above card.

Return books promptly to the Library or Temple Office.

Fines will be charged for overdue books or for damage or loss of same.

HOW TO LIVE
IN THE
PRESENT TENSE

HOW TO LIVE
IN THE
PRESENT TENSE

By Haim Kemelman

South Brunswick and New York: A. S. Barnes and Company
London: Thomas Yoseloff Ltd

A. S. Barnes and Co., Inc.
Cranbury, New Jersey 08512

Thomas Yoseloff Ltd
108 New Bond Street
London W1Y OQX, England

ISBN 0-498-07677-6
Printed in the United States of America

To Esther,
*who shared my work
and cheered my progress*

To David and Dina,
who shared and cheered us both

To Hinda,
who showed me the path of life

To Jacob,
*of blessed memory,
whose ladder stretched heavenward*

CONTENTS

ACKNOWLEDGMENTS

I WISH TO EXPRESS GRATITUDE TO MY HELPMATE IN LIFE, Esther, who helped me along every step of the way and turned my illegibly scribbled thoughts into the typed page and later into the typed manuscript; to my first editor, Mr. Alexander Jones, Editor of *The Daily Home News,* whose sensitivity and humanity guided my pen and encouraged my first literary efforts; to *The Daily Home News* for making theirs my home of reflection and introspection; to my friends Mr. Irving Lopatin, Editor of the Hayden Publishing Co., and Dr. Abraham Resnick, Professor of Social Studies, Jersey City State College, for their advice and technical assistance; to those newspapers where my column "Lines on Living" has appeared, for permission to use previously printed material; to Dr. Harold Fein, for his tireless devotion and help; to Attorney Charles Vaughn, of sainted memory, for past inspiration and loving encouragement; and to my many friends, the good people of the East Brunswick Jewish Center, whose encounters in faith and in life made my work possible. I am also indebted to loyal and thoughtful readers, from far and near, whose kind letters have spurred me on to this effort.

H. K.

HOW TO LIVE
IN THE
PRESENT TENSE

Listen to the Exhortation of the Dawn!
Look to this Day, for it is Life—
The very Life of Life!
In its brief course lie all the Verities
And Realities of your Existence:
The Bliss of Growth,
The Glory of Action,
The Splendor of Beauty;
For Yesterday is but a Dream,
And To-morrow is only a Vision;
But To-day well lived
Makes every Yesterday a Dream of
    Happiness,
And Every To-morrow a Vision of Hope.
Look well, therefore, to this day!
Such is the Salutation of the Dawn.

Unknown, *The Salutation of the Dawn.*
From the Sanscrit.

1.

IN GOODS WE TRUST

Be still, and know that I am God.
—*Psalms, 46, 10*

IS PEACE OF MIND WORTH HAVING? OBVIOUSLY, YOU'LL say. What can be more coveted than the inward peace of a serene disposition?

Yet today, when we see how the peace of mind cult turns into what A. Roy Eckhardt calls religious narcissism, peace of mind may well be misplaced and misapplied. Mindless peace may at best be no peace at all, or even worse: self-delusion.

Perhaps religion today is suffering because we have created a syndrome of wholesale dispensation of synthetic serenity and bliss at cut-rate prices in the form of relaxation and passive retreat. When people take Compoz for repose, relaxation for serenity and tranquilization for meditation, hallowed bliss becomes physical surrender and self-brain-washing. And the wisdom of prophetic admonition comes to mind warning us that peace can be illusive and deceptive, "Saying: Peace, peace; when there is no peace."

Inward peace is not a surrender to outward inducements but to the innermost feelings and impulses that are ours freely and that alone can make us free and serene. It is not in what we have and in what we possess, but in what we inwardly feel and for what we stand, that we will find our equanimity. Because if we cannot be contented with what

13

we are, what comfort can we find in all that we have, in a world of mushrooming goods, where we can always suffer discontent by comparison and covet what we see elsewhere.

A false sense of contentment is worse than discontent; mental peace that is mindless and smug is more troublesome than no peace at all. Because in the first instance there is struggle and hope, whereas in the latter, there is only opiating delusion and submission.

There is a healthy tension, a creative discontentment in all of us that sets us apart from the chewing animal and drives us onward and forward to our true human destiny. A dead person is totally relaxed; a broken clock is relieved of the tension of its mainspring; a sheep is contented in bleating and eating. Not man, the "unfinished animal." And all those spiritual soothers who offer a simple blueprint for peace of mind to avoid the normal tensions, feelings and problems of everyday life are false prophets of a compressed bliss and peace.

Are we today paying the price of a spirituality that offers serenity and peace of mind at discount prices? Is the drug syndrome of our time a direct offshoot of the mentality of a neat packaged gift of happiness and joy, peace and divinity, easily obtained in a formula?

What we need is not passive peace of an emotionless mind, but a dynamic and engaging peace that will give us the mental tuning and balance to leap into an encounter of humanity and divinity that will fire our imagination, spark our enthusiasm and brighten our vision. Total relaxation is for the dead. Absolute peace is in the grave. Complete contentment is for the lower animal—not man. And peace of mind is not a ticket to self-effacement.

To be reasonably tense and to enjoy it, that's excitement; to be nobly discontented and to glimpse higher sights, that's revelation; to be serenely dissatisfied with what is, because of vision as to what ought to be, that's humanity, divinity, prayer—life at its highest.

The desert manna, far from being a source of content-ment and gratitude, turned out to be a boring and stinting food to its consumers. Not because it was tasteless, but because it was effortless in attainment, inducing complacent living and dullness. Because it was too colorless, too good and too opiating, it caused frustration, boredom and a yearn-ing for bondage.

Therefore, if we crave for peace of mind that is not lulling ambition and dulling the senses, let it be like a prayer that is gentle while it moves mountains—that leads in serenity and offers the kind of repose that in its inner core of yearn-ing contains a splendid discontent that lights the world.

Unfortunately, however, this age that has made of con-venience a culture and of comfort a civilization, has also substituted respectability for respect and elegance for rev-erence. We seem to have gone awry somewhere. Success is not serenity, self-importance is not self-respect, and peace of mind is not mindless apathy. We know it, our children feel it and we all suffer for it.

With all our gadgets and riches, our science and luxury, we have failed to establish a certainty, a truth, a faith, upon which we can rely and upon which our children can repose. Many of us have given them a richness of things and our-selves a poverty of sophistication that touches only the sur-face of their lives and hardly answers the "deep unto deep," in our own curious existence.

Can it be that we have become so deficient in our faith that after losing faith in God, we have lost faith in ourselves and in each other? And having lost faith, we have also lost face. For when self-respect suffers, respectability is a victim; when our credibility is poor, our credit is low; when our vision is dim, our sights are narrow.

Perhaps this is what Robert Browning meant when he spoke of the need for "grasping the skirts of God." If the mini-skirted fashion of our time is emblematic of the short-cuts of our age, we can understand the necessity for "grasping the skirts of God," for a deeper faith in divine redemption, for a greater reverence for life's potential, for a fuller surrender to serene trust.

There is a need to restore human values, to revitalize hallowed traditions, to bring back individual dignity into our mass humanity. We cannot go back into the past. But neither can we run away from our family traditions, from our ancestry, from ourselves. This generation cannot turn its back upon the heritage of generations past. Not all ancient is holy and not all modern is good; not all old is outmoded and not all new is innovation. Often, the latest tune may prove nothing more than the replay of a broken record from a discarded past. Some of our values are blemished. Many of our concepts are confused. Many of our fashions go back to primitive times.

THE DIAL-A-MESSAGE SYNDROME

The temptation to offer discount salvation, wholesale redemption and quick answers to complex human problems is not new. We have listened for a long time to the prophets of peace and serenity telling us of the tranquilizing creed of relaxation that is made easy to come by in a self-induced passivity. Now there is something new added on the market. Dial-A-Prayer has gained a new companion in ministry. It's the Dial-A-Message for comfort and solace, and it has become big business. Thus we see not only business becoming a religion with some people, but also religion becoming a business with others.

This new system of "religious communication" makes use of the instant impulses of electronic gear by making it possible for its user to gain immediate access to the honey-dripping voice of the cleric—tape recorded and delivered—Parson to Person. Like the Dial-A-Prayer device, this remote control operation promises the individual never to be left alone in time of need, always gaining the earphone of hallowing human sound. At the same time, it offers the clergyman the convenience and dispatch of a quick and valuable service, sparing him the time and physical effort of a personal visit by simply making a congregant move his fingers along the yellow pages and dial a message of reassurance. In short, it's effectual and efficient.

What a feat of modernity! What an accomplishment of instant communication! What a triumph of the machine! But, for God's sake, who needs it?

The desire for anchorage, for a firmer support inherent in prayer and spiritual yearning, will not be turned on by a dial. The quest for refuge and certainty in the midst of life's uncertainties and in the roaring flux of things will not be answered by mechanical incantation, repeating a prayer like a broken record. The longing of one's individual frail self to merge into the corporate whole of God and man will not be fulfilled by being wired to sound. The soul will still remain unfulfilled. For communion with the Divine is not communication by dial; prayer efficacy is not instant efficiency, and faith cannot be packaged and delivered C.O.D.

Haven't we been mocked enough by the machine that has often replaced the personal touch of humanity, the warmth of the living individuality with robot-like insensitivity and impersonality? Why allow the machine to mock God and man by delegating to it the most sublime and intimate of human yearnings—our need to find oneness in the strong arms of the everlasting?

The most precious things in life don't come our way by the asking, and are certainly not advanced by proxy. If prayer and spiritual introspection means anything to us at all to be valuable, it is in its self-application and self-extension. It isn't perfunctory lip-service; it isn't mechanical superstition and magical enchantment. It is a service of the heart, a dynamic stirring of person and personality, awakening a unity and an identity and a sense of oneness with all divine. It is a person to person, person to God relationship—not a mechanical hook-up.

Too much perfume, someone has keenly observed, is in bad taste; and even the scent of sanctity can be overdone. This is especially true when sanctity is turned on by wire, by sound, by commercial means.

The acoustics of prayer are not best echoed in wired sound and in instant delivery; the sweet mellow message of faith is not best conveyed in a telephone dial and in a tape replay; the comforting thoughts of human sympathy are not best ministered by remote control.

Prayer, introspection and human sympathy can best be advanced in self-service, both of ministering parson and of individual person. And while it takes individual character to know for what we stand, it takes personal fortitude to know before whom we stand. Both are human qualities, not mechanical responses.

SELLING THE SOUL TO POT

And while religious mechanical hook-up is mediocrity, chemical turn-on can be disastrous. There are those who would induce instant mysticism in a strange and weird way reminiscent of primitive pagan witchcraft. They would go so far as to use a marijuana incense-ritual as "a significant vehicle to self-realization," and to the creation of a certain euphoric high conducive to instant mysticism.

Here, then, is the rub: instant mysticism. Any doctrine that makes mysticism instant, self-realization quick, divine revelation a bargain, is reverting to the dark ages when the neat package of a "heaven" was giftwrapped in a home-made glistening idol.

What a divine fraud: a pot-puffer is no prophet and an addict is no closer to revelation than the skid row drunkard, in spite of his momentary high, briefly induced by the tender mercies of drugs. Because the higher he "rises" the harder he falls and the deeper he sinks into the hell of his own making.

On a store window in the East Village a notice is posted: "One week's vacation to freak out—to rest our sore brains." But many who take the first trip never return. They go on a vacation that may last a week, a month, a year, a lifetime of individual retreat, personal waste and human shrinkage.

No, addiction is no sin. Worse than that, it's a crime. It's shackling one's own soul to a ritual reminiscent of ancient paganism and human bondage. For if it is a crime to kill a human being, it's equally a crime to smother a human soul, a creative intelligence, a free and unbounded life.

Man is man, emblazoned with the divine image, not for his freedom to sink back into the mire of animal life, uncontrolled and muddled by passion, power and lust; he is man for his ability to exert upon his life the higher disciplines which alone can promise the deeper joys and inspirations of life and human destiny.

For if religious faith means anything, it is to buttress

individual consciousness in the fullest meaning of life's reality, in depth and in comprehension, not to circumvent it by the detour of unreality, of escape and of liberation from responsibility and care by a false sense of ecstasy. There is enough substance in religious experiences, if practiced aright, to cheer the soul; enough excitements in life to amuse our curious nature; and enough of God's work to divert us from any thought of retreat and from selling our soul to chemical bondage. No liquid chemistry can be a worthy substitute for the spiritual chemistry of man. Salvation's promise surely must be greater than the addict's needlehead.

But the great weakness of our age lies in a tempestuous instantism—instant love, instant power, instant everything. We are prone to substitute the artificial for the real, the illusory for the authentic. Artificial inspiration is more self-deception than self-service. And you can't go on double-crossing yourself indefinitely.

When future historians will look back upon this age, they will most probably be intrigued by what one English writer calls our double thinking about God. Do we really double think about God? Is our profession of faith sincere, with words matched by deeds? Is our sense of morality, spirituality and values communicative and convincing?

If motion is an index of life and vitality, our age should abound in faith and bliss. The edifice complex of religious functional architecture is mushrooming. Ceremonial rite, with robe, ritual and splendor, is on the ascendancy. Yet, as we invoke God's name and offer our blissful incantations, we know that not infrequently there is something missing in all that we do, or say, or feel, or think. Can it be that we double think about God?

To many it has become a comfortable routine; they invoke the name of God so as to glimpse the halo of sanctified glow; but inside the soul there remains a hollow emptiness. Their children are entranced by the incense of other altars, stranger fires and heavier spices. They prostrate themselves at the mercies of drugs rather than the grace of the Almighty and worship the gods of pleasure and voluptuousness.

CHILDREN ARE RUNNING

"Everything is Now, everything is Today," is the watchword of their creed. And "now" and "today" shatter all meaningful reality of human experience and discipline, which alone can make the joys of living more than a fleeting blown-up syllable of time dipped in chemical witchcraft— unreal, unrelated and unthinking.

The shocking truth, however, is that countless youth, bright and good people, are bent upon mixing drug chemistry with their human chemistry; they begin by sniffing glue and gulping cough syrup in their early teens; they then graduate into pot, leading the way to the gates of continual descent into a private hell of their own making, by selling their souls to powder bliss. But why do they do their undefinable thing and in the process lose their definable self? Because they are reaching out in quest of something. They are in a contagion of conscience and mind. They seek a self-realization that has heretofore escaped them—a salvation unglimpsed, a redemption unexperienced. Something, apparently, is missing in the quality, the spirituality of their home life to make them so desperately unfulfilled. For when ideals vanish, idols emerge and the smelling salts of tinseled self-worship take over. For man is a worshipping animal. If he worships not something higher than himself, he comes to worship himself.

The source of ferment then, is not with the bliss-inhaling, pot-puffing youth of the turned-on generation. Something must have gone sour long before, as we have offered them a faith that has fallen on deaf ears, a self-confidence that has turned into self-defeat, a trust that has rusted into fractious contagion.

Don't you see, our children are running. They are often running at considerable risk, leaving what they consider empty affluence for fuller meaning. The running is frequently and shockingly reversed: not from tattered rags to promising riches, but from boring riches to escapist rags. Have we been too permissive, too superficial, too busy to do our "homework" in making the home more than a house, more than a motel, by failing to build it into a sanctuary of love and friendship, closeness and togetherness, warmth and faith? Have we been double thinking about God, double talking about ourselves and double crossing to our children?

Again we cannot fail recalling the prophetic admonition: "The fathers have eaten sour grapes and the children's teeth are set on edge." The disquieting and disturbing questions directed toward middle class America today must give us pause.

We must have gone sour somewhere. We must have somehow strayed from the path of righteousness that our ways seem so strange to the next generation and our children so estranged from us. Why, with all the panoply of our clerical authority, our educational processes and the sanctimonious rites of our religious institutions, have we come to witness the baleful alienation of so many of our young who have to turn on to a paganism of communal rites as a substitute worship that offers them, if only briefly and fleetingly, the salvation and the tender mercies of drugs! Why?

Is it possible that we are somewhat out of tune with our

faith? That we have put our trust in God but only in our spare time, which is most infrequent and most casual, leaving us unfulfilled and often bored?

THE NECESSITY FOR MENTAL TUNE-UP

For Killer No. 1 is not, as doctors have it, man's mortal enemy—heart disease. It's really mind disease. Because mental health has a way of affecting our total health and well being.

Boredom, for instance, literally kills a person by stripping him of his human initiative and the ability to live as a creative person. Excessive anxiety and undue worry can bring a man to the brink of war, a war with himself that has dire consequences of leaving its marks in ulcers, high blood pressure, heart trouble and other ailments.

Perhaps Dr. Carl Jung was not so wildly exaggerating when he asserted that among all the patients he treated, 35 years of age and over, "there hasn't been one whose problem in the last resort was not that of finding a religious outlook in life." In contemporary terms this means that lack of an identity and anchorage in some certainty can leave a person not only drifting and listless but also bruised and scarred. Mental attunement to the human "machinery" is what a car tune-up is to a motor. It brings the many parts of the body into smooth operation to affect total performance and efficiency. A few corroded spark-plugs can disable all of a car's combustible power.

How do we obtain the necessary mental tune-up?

By dialogue. Therapeutic faith provides for this dialogue that one must always maintain with himself, if he is to find himself in proper mental balance and spirit. Prophetic religion tells man: Tune-in on the indwelling spirit within you so that you remain tuned-up to the maximum performance of your capabilities as a creative human being.

There is the constant need in life to adjust to change outside yourself and inside of you. You are not today what you were yesterday and you must ready yourself to be tomorrow what you aren't today. Perhaps the greatest resentment we have to change is the change that occurs within us. But we must be realistic. It's no shame to admit that we have frailties and imperfections, waning powers and weaknesses to cope with, the major one of which is coping with ourselves in terms of an identity and personal destiny. There is a great deal of truth in what Dr. William Menninger said that "Mental health problems do not affect three or four out of every five persons, but one out of one."

However, if we can maintain a healthy dialogue with ourselves on a steady day-to-day basis, we can avoid a credibility gap creeping into our lives.

There is the credibility gap in the gulf that separates promise from performance, intent and deed, in what we expect of ourselves and what we are realistically capable of doing.

You must adjust, is a truism that we learn from our childhood and throughout life. Adjust to the world, we are constantly reminded. But there is another truism that lies at the heart of religion telling us to adjust the world to us as well: to shape it in the image of our dreams, to set standards of excellence (as far as we are individually capable) and personal experience. Don't be a joiner for the sake of status and class symbol. Be yourself, with yourself, for yourself, if you're to be any good with others and for others. If you know not how to love yourself, how can you possibly love your neighbor?

Adjustment is a two-way avenue for the individual. If he

adjusts totally to his society he is merely a human robot. If he demands the world to adjust totally to him, he is either a genius or insane. Most people are neither. They therefore must consider mental attunement as the No. 1 challenge of life and find the middle road in adjustment. They must constantly adjust to the outside world; but at the same time adjust the outside world to their inward humanity and faith. Because they are individuals with private worlds of dreams and visions and legitimate personal yearnings and destinies.

The ancient book of Proverbs tells us what we all know from personal experience, namely that "a soft answer turneth away wrath." And a gentle question will invite a soft answer.

The contemplative qualities of turning toward an inwardness of serenity and thought are missing in our lives. And we find the wisdom of the ancients evermore closer to the psychological realities that make of contemplative dialogue not only a spiritual luxury but a life necessity, an imperative of sane living.

"How can you expect God to speak to us in that gentle voice which melts the soul," asked F. Fenelon more than 300 years ago, "when you make so much noise with your rapid reflections? Be silent and God will speak again."

Today, 300 years later, the same question can be asked, only with greater intensity and urgency. For today our reflections are electric and our words garbled. We dance to the tunes of strange music; we hear the clatter of machines, the clamor of shouting masses, the rattle of lashing tongues. Banished is the still small voice, the power of gentleness, the spirit of peace.

What sleep is to the body, silence is to the mind. We need more hours of tongue-rest, more moments of solitude and quietude to rest beside the "still waters" of hushed serenity and comfort.

In our silence, "God will speak again," and we shall hear.

2.

DADDY, WHAT ARE YOU DOING WITH MY WORLD?

One father is more than a hundred school-masters.
—George Herbert

A LITTLE BOY, SO THE STORY GOES, WAS GIVEN A WORLD globe as a holiday gift. Cherishing the gift of his private world, he placed it in a secure spot in his room. One night, his parents found themselves debating a point of geography and needed the globe for reference. The father quietly tiptoed into his child's darkened room to reach out for the globe, when he suddenly heard the child's voice unexpectedly directed to him, "Daddy, what are you doing with my world?" This blunt and innocent question of the child turned the father's thoughts that night from reference points of geography to thoughts of philosophy.

"What are you doing with my world?" asks the child. Are you going to hand over to me a fat allowance with a meager allotment of time of family togetherness? Are you going to fill my room with mechanical toys and leave my heart empty by unfulfilled cravings of the spirit? Are you going to secure for me an education to make a living, without the inspiration to prepare for life? Are you going to bestow upon me a world of things to have without a world of things to do?

"Daddy, what are you doing with my world?" asks the

child. Are you going to endow me with the example of love by your acts of love and consideration to mother? With the example of truth, by unfailing loyalty, fidelity and family devotion? With the example of kindness, by the sincerity of charity and grace? With the example of constancy, by steadfast faith and steady hands? Or are you, daddy, just going to be the father-pal showering solicitous over-protection in a faceless homogenized world of stifling conformity? Are you going to be my father, the man to inspire loyalty, to guide in righteousness, to uplift in spirit and to set standards —to pass on to me not just worldly goods but the good that you yourself are? "Daddy, what are you doing with my world?"

* * *

Children are very much on parents' minds at all times. We are constantly given to thoughts and reflections, secret hopes and fears on the ages-old, awe-inspiring preoccupation of parents: the business of rearing children. We are naturally concerned with our children's education. We worry about their grades and their personalities, their progress and development. We are reminded that "How to talk to the child," can make the difference between a happy home life and a battlefield. Because children, being human and also children, have "mixed-up feelings," they are easily hurt. Therefore, we are advised that if we handle them with firmness and finesse, consistency and tact, we will better be able to communicate with them.

No question, there is a great deal of merit to this. We know from our own experience how often we fail in our communication with one another, not because of the content of our words but because of the context of our pitch, of high tension and of nagging frequency. But more important than what we say to the child is what we are to the child.

"Children," C. G. Jung aptly tells us, "are educated by what the grown-up is and not by his talk." That is to say, that in our attitudes and values of life we form the mirror in which the child's own character and personality may be reflected and molded—for good or for evil. Character development, desirable traits and habits, are not the result of sweet talk alone, but the consequences of that intangible first and best school of life: home. Here, attitudes and values, examples of loyalty and devotion, faith and kindness, are interwoven into the fabric of actual living. Here, "how to live" is a more convincing example to the child than "how to talk," and mutual reciprocity and closeness speaks to his heart more clearly than smooth words and nice talk.

Experiences—meaningful and elevating experience of parents and children together—are the basis for wholesome communication with the young. And this can be achieved in no other place than in the home, the living fountain of ideals and warmth, of discipline, faith and fortitude. The home is, and remains, the house of communication, the clearing house to the child, where attitudes of life are not "taught" in words but "caught" in habits of actual living. In such a home the whole of the child is developed. The training then becomes a fusion of personality integration, not merely the perfunctory child education that makes its supreme purpose the stuffing of so many "dos" and "don'ts."

The best method of teaching is by example and precept; by what we are, not by what we want our children to be; by what we mean to them, not by what we say to them; by how we relate to them, not by what we give them. Our primary gift to them must be ourselves, the example of our own lives. The pal idea of togetherness between father and son may be good, up to a point. But there comes a time in the child's life when he wants more than a 35-year-old pal.

He is guided more by emulation than by education. He looks for inspiration, guidance, steadfast hands and shining examples as a means of molding his own life.

Because the business of bringing up children deals with the future generation, no easy formula can be applied for its successful execution. The only safe rule about it is that when dealing with children, we must first begin with ourselves. For our example and the contents of our home living, will leave immortal impressions upon our children. As in the words of Daniel Webster: "If we work upon marble, it will perish; if on brass, time will efface it; if we rear temples, they will crumble into dust; but if we work upon immortal minds, and imbue them with principles, with the just fear of God and love of our fellowmen, we engrave on those tablets something that will brighten to all eternity."

FULL TIME PARENTHOOD

To assure wholesome consistency and unity of purpose in the home, equal involvement of both parents is required. Father and mother should be equally involved, never delegating the responsibility only to one parent because the other parent is too preoccupied with other responsibilities and problems.

There are those fathers who feel that their only burden of responsibility lies in making a living. They thus abdicate the involvement of rearing children and leave it entirely to the mother. The bread-winner often finds himself to be the home-loser because his concern and interest, his energies and talents are exclusively invested outside the home. Such people may be considered successful individuals in the outside world, but alas, dismal failures at home.

But what is really a father? Perhaps we'd better start by

saying what a father is not. A father is not a parent by absenteeism, who gives his child everything—everything money can buy—except the priceless gift of himself, his time and his sharing of experiences. A father is not the Benevolent Society man who stays in town and spends his evenings bowling and clubbing, "that to all practical purposes for the family, he might just as well stay in town and mail the paycheck home." A father is not what he does and gives the child, but what he is and means to the child. The supreme test of a father is whether he can inspire love by the love he evinces to his family; whether he can inspire loyalty and truth by his steadfastness and rootage in the home; whether he can inspire faith and honesty by his personal conduct and conviction.

The healthiest and most wholesome approach to parenthood is a unity of purpose in the home and singleness of direction in the raising of children. Children are influenced by attitudes more than by words. And the attitudes of home living, in the end, are the most determining factors in deciding what kind of parents we are and what sort of children we raise.

It is not good when one parent contradicts the other in front of the child. It only confuses the child and weakens his sense of direction. Children are fair and willing to be useful partners in the family and act responsibly, provided that consistency and not contradiction is the rule of the home. Fairness and consistency in the home is more than good policy; it's the foundation of peace and growth, trust and understanding. It is not good for the mother to be the soft liberal and excessively easy with the child, constantly calling upon the father in the last resort to become the strict disciplinarian, the law and order candidate.

The united sense of a togetherness and fairness of home-living should be so strong and love-living so dominant that the child would never fail to get this point across: "I love you always, but sometimes I don't love the way you act."

Children are willing to take criticism and discipline offered in the constructive setting of communication and sensible reasoning. Such guidance will not be bruising to the child and will never leave the scars of either withdrawal or resentment in the child. But the great dilemma of our age is communication. We seem to communicate miraculously from the moon but somehow find it difficult to communicate in our home with our children. Why? Apparently because we have failed in our homework at home.

The trend of our time is running. To be sure, it is running for a good reason: to make a living, to make money and more money and more. Ironically, the children of affluence now reject the reason for their parents' running. They are in search of a cause. Yet, the compounded tragedy is that they too are running. It's time to come home. Father come home, come home! The children are waiting with that most magical word in their mouths: Daddy. For father is a hero figure at home, a model. And children look for heroes to emulate. They "have more need of models than of critics." Yet, to many of them, parents are all-out strangers and uninvited critics and the only models they see are those television characters, blown-up myths, unreal, and unworthy of emulation.

There was a time, not too long ago, when the family was a closely knit unit of endearing and enduring unity, with real-life experiences shared by all. There might have been little luxury in the home, but there was much solace; little of comfortable things, but much comfort; little riches of belongings, but great wealth in belonging; little gift-giving, but much life-sharing, self-giving.

There were even times when the stomach was half empty, but never the soul! There was a richness of spirit in the midst of poverty, a fullness of joy in the midst of trial, a heart-touching warmth and solidarity that made the great parent a humble friend and the small child a great participant. With all the knocks and bumps of life, they were together, enduring and persevering, always protecting their inner line of defense, the home, from which there could be no retreat. Here, the fondest hopes and dreams were nestled, in spite of all evil and tribulation. And they came out the stronger, the better, the nobler.

Children in such a home atmosphere were real partners in the purest and noblest sense of participatory family living. Even the disciplines that were often rigid didn't alienate the young and didn't sever the family bond of loyalty to traditions and values. The family, perpetuating heritage, remained the holy of holies upon whose altar no time was spared and no sacrifice was too precious. The daily ritual of living together endowed the home with the qualities of a sanctuary—not a place to run away from, but a retreat to run into for the refueling of strength, spirit, stamina and fortitude.

SPLIT-LEVEL FAMILY LIFE

What is the modern home today, what is the quality of family living? Is it split-level living and housing within a spacious and sumptuous edifice? There is obviously too much space between parents and children, too much room for estrangement, too many walls of separation and schism. Are we so wired to outside sound, tumult and clatter that we fail to communicate within the family and with our children?

There is much verbal and visual violence on television that cannot fail but leave ugly impressions and warts upon the child's soul. And in the absence of meaningful family living and involvement, the child is abandoned to the "vacuum cleaner" of time, a tube that enwraps and enraptures him in a world of outsized life characters, often distorting reality and causing mental violence.

True education of children is reciprocal: we not only educate our children, they educate us as well. And the original meaning of discipline comes from the Latin which means "to teach." The discipline of punishment, "do as I say," is futile, hypocritic and unconvincing. It causes bitterness and, in the end, alienation and total estrangement. The discipline of instruction is coupled with example and precept: "do as I do." This needs little enforcement and draws the family together in a bond of mutual living, enduring habit and destiny.

Do you want to teach your child manners, honesty, truth, devotion, loyalty, love and respect? Act it! Do it yourself! Children are good mimics, excellent imitators; and they will unfold fully with all the grandeur of their imagination and vision to all that is real, true and sincere in our life. No wonder, the biblical verdict is harsh and merciless in reminding us that the iniquities of fathers are visited upon their children. In this startling judgment, we realize that the film of our own life may have a re-run in the lives of our children, a repeat performance. They take on our bruises or perpetuate our glory. And this may turn out to be parents' greatest punishment or reward, defeat or triumph, as they see the seeds they have planted—by being what they are— grow into the full bloom of their children's life.

The challenge confronting many parents today is the cry within the home for reconstruction. There is a need to revitalize home traditions and values and turn them into potent factors of influence upon our children. The stress for personality development is hardly enough. To open the way of the world for the child, to prepare him for a living is only half the job. Equally important is to open the child to the ways of the world, to prepare him for life. Parents today have a right to be concerned with the quality of education their children receive, the kind of staff the school employs, the sort of textbooks their children will use. But they should be interested in something infinitely more than making of their children repositories of factual material and hoarders of book-stuff. They ought to be anxious to see their children develop their humanity so that they will ultimately blossom forth into decent and creative individuals, well-rounded, happy and adjusted. They must think not only of what their children will have in terms of educational opportunities but most of all what they will turn out to be in their human development and in their attitudes toward life—in growing up right, in doing right, and in the right way.

GENERATIONS APART

Parents today remember those other parents of a generation earlier, parents who ran from rags to riches, promising themselves that their children would never know material want and educational poverty. But all didn't turn out right. For they guarded against every conceivable poverty except poverty of the spirit. They gave their children everything—everything money can buy—big allowances, little worry, ample security, the best schooling and a key to the car. But they often failed to give them the key to life. They were free and open, with hand and heart, in preparing their children for a living, but alas, not in preparing them for life.

Freedom, education and security were the key words in

the upbringing of children and in preparing them to take their place in our society. But many of them copped out even while being equipped with freedom, education and security. They rebelled against the affluence that fed them. Freedom turned from a positive choosing and identifying with a set of options into a run-away rejection of everything that has to do with the past and with all traditional values.

Security was always the major consideration for a college education. But now we find that the richly educated feel and act not so secure and strong, and an academic insurance premium is no foolproof assurance to a successful adult career. What really counts, we come to realize as we never did before, is the humanity and personal growth into which our children develop as mature and responsible individuals. The mood of living and the attitudes of life, faith and human inner-directedness are as crucial in making life as knowledge and education are important in making a living. What children need is more than textbooks, text-teachers and black-boards. They need full-time parents.

You want to be a pal to your child? You will hardly make it by virtue of your age and interest gap. You want to be a parent to your child? There's your chance. Be a full-time parent, spending time with your children: leading and guiding, by example of living, by inspiration, and not by dictation and repression. Be all the parent you can be so that your child can grow into all the man he has the potential of being. There can be a happy partnership in home living where the lines of communication are open, where love and trust reside within the home-fortress, instead of mistrust and alienation.

Because there is such amplified electric shock music among youth with a magnetic cacophony and conformity of its own, the need for communication and dialogue in the home is all the more important. And the time to talk things over is not only when problems emerge, when passions are inflamed and reason is impaired. The occasion to communicate with children is not to wait until a crisis has developed, but to maintain an open line of calm dialogue, reason and trust among members of the family at all times.

The school will, at best, impart an education to our children but not attitudes of life and the basis for their healthy personal development and anchorage. This is the kind of homework that must be accomplished in the home, with parents and children hard at work to do that which cannot be delegated to any other person or place.

If parents deserve the kind of children they have, then parents have little reason to cheer about these days. For the ancient judgment of the visitation of the sins of the fathers upon their children is not arbitrary biblical justice, but the relevant and bitter reality of today. In the malaise of the young generation of our children are reflected the sins of the older generation, of omission and commission.

Where have we gone wrong, ask many parents when they discover the shock of their children's estrangement from their homes, their parents' traditions and values. What have we done to have deserved this runaway heartbreak, this generation gap?

Well, to begin with, the generation gap is a two-way gulf that has steadily and increasingly widened on both sides of the gaping chasm that presently separates the generations of parents and children. And if many youths run today, they must have discerned in us the pattern of running long before. What have we been doing, where have we been running—toward what direction, purpose, and end? We have run from the negative, but have we also pursued the positive? This generation fled from the pain of poverty and the shame of want, resolving that grinding poverty is an evil that must be eradicated. Running had become an end in itself; arriving in the economic sense was considered ultimate redemption.

But now we know it is not enough. Because our society may increasingly rise in status and affluence and still remain poor in spirit, bored in convenience and depressed in luxury. Because if there is no material depression today, there is a spiritual depression, a mental depression that commenced with the syndrome of the tranquilizer, the first legitimatized and glorified prescribed drug. And life can become habitually and aimlessly an evanescence of escape instead of an enticing arena of encounter: the molehills of daily problems can turn into overshadowing mountains to be feared and avoided by taking the more sedating road of the pill, a detour and short cut on the journey of living.

Medicine chests become private drug stores with a wide variety of pills of many colors, drugs for every purpose: against exuberance, against depression, against too little happiness, against too much happiness. In short, the pill, instead of being the remedy to redeem from pain and ailment, turns into pain and ailment itself, a chemical crutch robbing the individual person of his self-redeeming and self-helping powers that the addicted will seldom again come to tap for self-recovery.

A prominent scholar and educator pointed out recently that in order to cure student unrest, we will have to gain adult unrest. By this he meant that a certain creative restlessness is what gives life purpose and direction and our society meaning and vision. For too long have we listened to the messages of soothing spiritual syrup: relax and live; be tranquil and have peace of mind. But it no longer works. This generation echoes more the lament of Jeremiah: "Peace,

peace; when there is no peace," learning from bitter reality and disappointment that peace, inner and outer, is a dynamic attainment, not an induced gift.

There is a need today for a renaissance. There is a restlessness among the young in America for a new set of national purposes that will infuse people with a self-worth and narrow the gap between our professed ideals and our actual performance. We cannot say faith and mean fashion; religion and mean convenience; conscience and mean cowardice; tranquility and mean tranquilizer; joy and mean escape; adventure and mean self-mutilation; serenity and mean inertia; trust and mean money; confidence and mean insurance; dialogue and mean dualogue.

For when we narrow the credibility gap in our own hearts, we will surely be able to narrow the generation gap in our homes and "turn the hearts of the fathers upon the children and the hearts of the children upon their fathers." But heart alone is not enough, nor is love sufficient. A healthy understanding and mutual respect in the home is also necessary.

Many of us use the word love to cover up a lot of mischief. We speak of love in the home and love of children. But love is really beside the point. It is only an emotion, a sentiment; and there are healthy emotions and sick emotions. Love, too, can be sick and sickening. To be sure, love is what makes the home and love is the most important component of life, for us and our children. But love can be misguided, mismanaged and misspent. How much felicity can one shower without pampering, how much affection without spoiling? Love can also smother when it's a selfish expression of overextended parental mastery and servitude; for it can cause undue dependence upon parents.

True love is liberation and freedom, the release of personal fulfillment—not its subjugation. And if love demands the sacrifice of the individual spirit, it's a miscarriage. Because intelligent love requires of us to love not only with the heart but also with the mind. Love! But let live! Don't smother the sapling offspring with the giant shadows of your sprawling branches of overcoverage and overprotection.

The insights of modern psychology reveal to us the wisdom of emotion and feeling. When we love to domineer, to possess, to perpetuate our own ego in our offspring, we really love ourselves more than the child. The punishment to the child can be the lifetime penalty of having to grow into the kind of human Samuel Butler spoke of as being "compelled by unkind fate to parental servitude for life . . . a form of penal servitude" of the worst kind. Like anything good, love of children has to be planned and worked at deliberately and patiently. It's not a part-time job. And when we take a short-cut in the home, we take a detour to adequate parenthood—we cut short the childhood of our children that they desperately need.

Of all animal life, the human child is the slowest to develop into his own personality, independently. E. H. Erikson explains: "Human childhood is long, so that parents and schools may have time to accept the child's personality in trust and to help it to be disciplined and human in the best sense known to us." Childhood, then, is more than a transition time from non-man to man. It is the very incubation period for the future man. A healthy and wholesome childhood cannot be rushed.

Sadly, restlessness of haste and speed of our time, as in other spheres of life, has come upon childhood too. There is hardly a childhood for the child. Children today are left with themselves for long periods of time and when they see their parents, they find them tension-laden, anxiety-ridden. Thus, while a father says "I want my child to have the things I didn't have," he often leaves him without the thing he needs most—a fatherhood, a father real to the child in living and in relating. Perhaps some of these fathers who complain that nothing much was given to them as children, forget that they have been fortunate to gain a lot more than they are capable of giving their own children —the warmth of closeness and intimacy: the gift of a father who shares experiences to make the world of the child real and exciting. For one room of parenthood is worth more than a whole world of things, and one corner of a home is more precious than a sumptuous and empty house.

Too many children today have no childhood. They are pushed into maturity immaturely. The girl in her tiny teens who wears lipstick and a long gown, stumbling upon her high heels, is more often the expression of her mother's anxiety to see her daughter become popular, than the child's wish to masquerade in grown-up fashion. Respect your child's feelings is as much a sacred commandment as "Honor thy father and thy mother." Because the greatest honor that can come to parents is to see their offspring blossom into mature humanity by making whole human beings out of them; by making a home-life out of an empty house; by making a project of life out of childhood—never rushing it into the tumultuous world of grown-up problems.

*   *   *

The little figure, with her tiny hand waving, moved out of the house on a bright, early morning. She went to school, my three-year-old daughter. She was happy and she was afraid. For this was her first step in the big world, the first tiny leap all by her little self. Be kind to her, World. Show her that the sweet, innocent world she knows is real, even while she may have to work hard to discover it.

Be patient with my little girl, School of Life; be understanding to her, even when she cries her temperamental
tears of pampered childishness, even while she makes her
screaming demands. You see, we spoiled her a little; we
didn't mind it, in fact we enjoyed it. In the home, she was
boss. Everything she wanted in her young life—almost
everything—she took. But the world gives no one everything he wants. Teach her, therefore, that the wisdom of
life is to love what we have rather than to have everything
we love. Tell her, School of Life, patiently and lovingly,
that the world she will have will be the world of life she
will make—not what she will take from life, but what she
will give to life; not what she will grasp and hold, but
what she will perceive and experience; not what life will
do to her, but what she will do to life.

Teach my little girl, School of Life, what wiser loving
men have discovered a long time ago, that the sweetest and
most precious things of life come free and must be enjoyed
freely by brave spirits. And that those earned gifts are the
reward of stout hearts and willing hands. And if she wills
and dreams and longs long enough, she will never lose,
even if she is not victor. Because the fun of life is not so
much in having won, but in having dreamt, not in having
gained triumph, but in having tried to compete and to
excel. Winning isn't everything, but trying is. Just as
falling is no shame, but the unwillingness to rise again is.

Teach my little youngster, School of Life, to be honest,
to be true. Never mind the crooks, never mind the cheats,
never mind the bullies. The world is still full of people who
prize honesty above gold and gentleness above all power.
Teach her, therefore, to have faith in humanity, even if she
can't keep faith in all humans.

She will need faith. It will be everything in life to her.
Give her, then, faith in peace, in hope, in truth, in the

loveliness of life and light. Give her faith in herself: to believe that the individual makes a world of difference because one person, one soul is a whole world. Give her the wisdom to use that power of individuality to join the righteous cause; and the courage to defy evil even if she has to stand alone.

Teach her, School of Life, humility but not withdrawal; determination but not violence; bravery but not recklessness; gallantry but not defiance; freedom but not anarchy. And teach her to be respectful not only of the possessions of others but also of their dignity and person. Let her know that shouting is not dialogue and insult is no winning ace. Inform her that the still small voice is still the mightiest instrument and the lubricating oil of tenderness is still mightier than the fist.

Teach her, dear School of Life, that the greatest heartaches of life are not in the things we do, but in the things we leave undone, in the dreams that haven't been dreamt, in the smiles that haven't been awakened, in the friendships that haven't been evoked, in the love that hasn't been invoked—in all the thousands of little things that make the great life of man a joy or a regret.

And finally, dear, dear School of Life, be kind to my little girl and help her to be strong, for there is much to bear; to care, for there is much to do; to be brave, for there is much cowardice; to be true, for there is much hypocrisy —to find meaning in "I" and glory in "We".

How about it, School of Life? Can you do it? Try. I will do my best to try in my little School of Life—my home, my little girl's home.

3.

TURN-ON BY TUNING-IN ON LIFE

Where is the Life we have lost in living?
Where is the wisdom we have lost in knowledge?
Where is the knowledge we have lost in information?
The cycles of Heaven in twenty centuries
Bring us farther from God and nearer to the Dust.
　　　　　　　　　　—Thomas Stearns Eliot

IN A SELF-SHATTERING DISCOVERY OF A NEW AWARENESS, Ellen Sturgis Hooper observes a fundamental truth of life, declaring: "I slept and dreamed that life was beauty. I awoke—and found that life was duty." But where is the truth to be found? Is it in the dream of beauty or in the reality of duty? Perhaps life is both: beauty and duty, intermingled and fused in coexisting balance.

The most beautiful things in life, the most satisfying joys of living, the most gratifying experiences of consciousness, are nearest and freest to us. Money cannot buy them. They are obtained only by one's own self-redeeming powers, in the involvement of the duties of the heart and in the disciplines of the mind. Only by our conscious efforts and liberating toil can we discover them.

The universe is a dramatic stage of cosmic superlatives, of unfolding beauty. A blade of grass, a flower, a living organism—all have their roots in the sun and their unity with the stars. Everything is laden with the elements of motion and suspense, in a primal relationship within the grand chain of evolving creation. But universal beauty and unity demands the eye of the beholder, the mind of the conscious, the relatedness of the feelingful. "Next to beauty is the power of appreciating it," we are reminded. And if life is a book in which all of us can read a few lines to decipher meaning, it is incumbent upon us to train our eyes to the mystifying pages of the eternal, universal volume of creative reality—miracle of miracles. For how can we fail in seeing how "God writes the Book of Genesis every day."

We cannot all be masters of art and creators of beauty, but all of us can become the happy spectators to a panorama of wonder, an expanse of unimaginable spectacles staggering the imagination. Creation, in a stupendous attraction of "mighty opposites" in a constant state of flux, is at work —it's the unfinished business of the Eternal in time and space. And we, the people of intelligence, are given the treat of our lifetime: to be witness bearers to the worlds of creation outside us and to a world of divine intelligence inside us. And when we look and observe with the discerning eye, we see the drama of creation unfolding in all its splendored things. Raise but your keen eyelid and the curtain opens to the majestic and wonderous sights of endless magic.

We must therefore pray for open eyes to see; and when seeing to behold; and when beholding to discern and relate. The spectacle of the heavens—if we but look aright—cannot be matched by any art or stage of man. And the entrance ticket is only a willing perceptiveness that is cultivated and refined by the enthusiastic soul.

Those who desperately seek to turn-on, in quest of that

spurt of ephemeral moment of mystic euphoria, use a chemical reaction when they can be buttressed by their own spiritual chemistry. They only need the will and the zest to concentrate on themselves and tap their own human resources. It is a false prophecy and delusion that promises exhilaration at the price of a coin and spirituality in the underworld market. There is a heaven within the heart as real as the heaven of God, if the divine spirit resides within it, if beauty adorns it. The uncontrolled fire of turning on against one's self is explosive. The illuminating flame of tuning-in on forces greater than one's own is exalting and amplifying. There is a cogent power in reality for those who would decipher its meaning to find its real magic. The only thing it requires is an inward concentration, for self-enlarging and self-ennobling vitality, to tap enthusiasm for life at its very roots and in its simplest forms; to gain a relating intimacy to the origins whence we sprang to living intelligence; to inspire a confidence in the ultimate goodness which is at the source of heaven and man.

To lose one's self in himself, is to shrivel to the size of a drop of a milky maddening oblivion. To lose one's self in something higher than himself, is to grow in universal scope in quest of one Milky Way of one heaven after another. Ecstasy lies in hallowed vision unfolding to the eye. It is neither granted free, nor can it be injected freely. It is a relationship, not an escape; a reality, not an illusion; a lifetime journey, not a weekend "trip."

Any thrill and joy that is sought for its own sake will bring no lasting happiness and no enduring pleasure. It will crumble by turns in the nightmare of fear and in the smoke of misty oblivion and forgetfulness. The beauty of joy and fantasy must grow out of the duty of inner struggle, of daring adventure, of a life-consciousness that reaches out into the lives and loves of souls and sights, in time and in space. In its most glorifying reality, it will become a unifying force to merge cell and soul, to integrate time and space, to fuse beauty and duty into a union of oneness.

In the end, it is outgoing engaging duty, not retreating self-indulgent happiness-hunting, that will bring us the higher joys of the spirit and the deeper verities of ecstatic living. The high priests of chemical solace, the potion gobblers, the dial-a-salvation-and-see-God proponents, are self-deluding when they seek to crowd the fugitive moment with the eternity of a heaven. Drug chemistry is no substitute for human potency and instantism for mysticism. By breaking down the normal confines of time and space, they sow the seeds of personal disintegration and abandon their lives within the ruins of smoldering ashes. For the higher they float, the lower they plunge downward, to the stark reality of awakening, as they find themselves outsiders in a world of duty, responsibility and beauty.

When Elijah sought the Divine spirit, he found it not in the blaze-bursting lightning, neither in the power-crushing earthquake, nor yet in the energy-sweeping whirlwind. For it was in the still small voice of duty and in the sanctuary of his heart. Because greatness and Divine grace are not produced in abrupt, earth-shaking, spectacular and dramatic acts. They are the great works of the small rays of a life of sunshine, sprinkled with the countless drops of the rain of human kindness that lavish growth and warmth to the world. It is, summarily, in duty and in beauty.

"SO NIGH IS GRANDEUR TO OUR DUST . . ."

Whether our duties are great or small—in public life or in private enterprise, in making a living or in keeping a home, in the office or in the plant, in the classroom or in the boiler room—each and everyone of us can feel a sense of satisfaction in fulfilling his duties aright, whatever they may be. In such fulfillment we come to glimpse that beauty and truth which emerge in selfless involvement, social participation and human extension.

No one summed it up better than Emerson when he linked God to man in a binding commitment between the two: "So nigh is grandeur to our dust, so near is God to man, when duty whispers low, 'Thou must,' the youth replies, 'I can.'"

In the responsive prayer of "I can," a power is given to man to rise above himself. And there are prayers without words: prayers of silent devotion; prayers of mood rather than mouth. In the mystic insight of Berdichevsky, "All things pray, and all things exhale their souls. . . . Creation is itself but a sweetness and a longing, a sort of prayer to the Almighty, blessed be He."

A beautiful song, heartfelt devotion, the poetry of silence, the harmony of sound, color and shape—all are rooted in that longing of sweetness, which express a unity in creation, an adoration to the Creator. We can engage in this exciting encounter of song wherever we are: in the field and in the home, in the house of prayer and in the heart of meditation. Our openness can be as high as the sky. Emerson put it this way: "Never lose an opportunity of seeing anything that is beautiful; for beauty is God's handwriting—a wayside sacrament. Welcome it in every fair sky, in every fair flower, and thank God for it as a cup of blessing."

In such a creed of faith and an appreciation of nature, you become involved in a romantic experience of a lifetime. For life, then, speaks to you in a thousand voices: Awaken man! Sing a song, raise your voice, lift your spirit, soar above your shallow self. Embrace all the world in an encounter of faith, in a dialogue of sensitivness and perceptiveness. It will cheer your heart and brighten your soul. It will bring you revelations of the Divine, to inspire the prophet in you, the spark of foresight, the ember of insight. You'll find God residing in the joyous heart, in your simple self and soul. Speak to it and it will speak to you. Relate to it and it will answer you in the secret sounds of "the still small voice."

For if it is true that life is what we make of it, it is equally true that life is where we discover it. And we find it wherever we look for it. The world is a romantic stage of unfolding beauty, ceaselessly speaking to us in many scenes and acts and in countless revelations. We can be the happy crowd of individualities (not the faceless mass of tribal conformity) if we but attune ourselves to beauty in a ceaseless stirring and an awakening to life and by a tune-up to the inner harmonies of "the still small voice." For if we can stir all our life forces, we will come to release all our potential for the love of beauty and the love of life.

TURNING OFF THE DARKNESS

Man is a spatial and expansive creature. Alone, in retreat of his narrow confines, he is a recluse of loneliness and boredom, one of God's frailest creatures. Joined, however, in a chorus of response to the prayer and the longing within him and within the universe, he is the resplendent creature, crown of creation. And the more unity he can find within himself, the more universality he can evoke in response to the life forces of his human race and the outer space embracing him.

The strength of the beast is in its hidden bones of brute and muscle. It lives by the kill and dies for the killer.

Man's power is in his inner recesses of intelligence and soul. He lives in the flesh, but abides by the spirit and by mingling with the world. To live and let live is no longer enough for him. What he needs is human compassion and human comprehension. But, ah, there is the rub. For, as we are reminded, we find it much easier to love humanity as a whole, than to love humans individually, in relating experiences. And yet we recall the truth of him who said, "A man is like a letter of the alphabet. To produce a word, it must combine with another." But contemporary man's problems are compounded and amplified in that his writing is in shorthand and his letters are hardly legible; the individual character is so blurred and unrecognizable.

We have great lights in great cities. We have neon signs and flashy symbols. But they can be so cold and remote, uninspiring and unilluminating. There is a chilling loneliness in the air, a howling darkness in the gleam of electric light. For so many walk in darkness, so many are afraid in the light, so many are dazzled and blinded by the unremitting floodlights because they see not the hand above them that will help them on. Perhaps what we need is not so much to turn on lights in the streets, but to turn off the darkness in our hearts: the darkness that casts fear, that bruises, that divides, that crushes bodies and mutilates souls and leaves us with the identities of the morgue and the destinies of primitives. And, alas, darkness is so vast and the flame so frail and defenseless that only the vigil of the faithful will keep it alive.

A father once heard his child's frightened voice coming to him from the youngster's darkened bedroom: "Daddy, I'm afraid," cried the horrified child. "Turn off the darkness." Turning off darkness, however, is more than turning on a switch. It means to banish human loneliness, anguish, strife, fear, shame, degradation and hurt. And the lights that will turn off darkness in the heart are kindled by warm hands, by unfaltering faith and steadfast minds of comprehending humans. They are born in the glowing flames of grace, devotion and service; they are conceived in man's urgency to reach out for the stars and to relate within his own sphere and constellation of lives and lights.

This then is the message of the song of the human heart praying and longing for unity: Blessed is the flame that is eternal; the more it sheds of its own light, the more its sparks increase, the more its warmth spreads. Why "Curse the darkness"? Kindle a light! Yet, too many people are negative instead of being positive. With curse on their lips and darkness in their heart, they fail to see the light that will turn into a human flame of joy, of happiness and of gratitude. They fail in the encounter of human appreciation. They are negative in their thinking and thanking and are shrouded in the darkness of a melancholy soul. Ingratitude, sharper than a serpent's tooth, bites into their healthy lifestream to envenom its healthy functions.

For whatever we may have in abundance, let's face it, it's not gratitude. Whatever plenty we possess, it's not a feeling of thanksgiving. Henrik Ibsen's truth, uttered at the turn of the century, still haunts us today, reminding us that money may buy many things, but not everything.

Money can buy "food but not (an) appetite, medicine, but not health, acquaintances, but not friends." Money can buy a bed but not rest; pills but not salvation; comforts but not comfort; pleasure but not joy; convenience but not bliss; luxury but not sublimity; elegance but not respectability; makeup but not character; a good time but not a good conscience; success but not happiness; fortunes but not fortitude; security but not serenity; dividends but not divinity; leisure and time, but not the peace and thought-fulness to enjoy it.

COMPUTERS DON'T COUNT BLESSINGS

In the computer age, counting is turned over to the machine. But the computer can't count our blessings for us and register a "thank you" for providential care and bounty. Gratitude, like prayer, must come from the heart, from a recognition of life and a relatedness in living so total and absorbing as to make us respond "Amen" to the many voices in the universe speaking to us and stirring us to adoration, thanksgiving and devotion. However, because for too long we have been telling ourselves that things—position and possession—make the man and induce happiness and recognition, we now haplessly discover that they don't bring us human comprehension and perception, cultivation of character and an identity. We have even lost the human, all-too-human quality of according appreciation to ourselves—for what we are to ourselves and what we mean to one another. Too often we take one another for granted and shudder in embarrassment from a word of praise, appreciation and approval. We find it easier to flatter a stranger than to praise those who are near and dear to us. And so we find the song of our life frequently discordant because there are too many "flat" notes of ingratitude in our score.

When we fail in our thanksgiving, we fail in our thanks-being as well. And this is a failure of nerve and of heart rather than a failure of material insufficiency. For in the end, it's not in what we have that we find our contentment, but in what we think we have, as we extend our gratitude of appreciation for our gifts. And if dear ones and friends have one another and take time out to live and to love and enjoy each other, and express their mutual reciprocity, there is little more they need. In our better judgment (and at times it dawns upon us too late), we may realize that we possess a wealth that we use all too miserly—our acknowledged approval and expression of appreciation. It is a gift that comes in small packages but it turns up in huge bundles of joy to the receiver as well as to the giver. It comes in a warm smile, in honest praise, in a note of thanks, in a word of encouragement, in a gesture of comfort, in a soft blessing, in a fervent prayer.

It takes little effort but it has priceless value and depth. And so many of us can use it. So many hunger for acceptance, for approval, for a nod of encouragement. But, alas, we hold it back and stifle it in dead silence. We are so loud to blame, but so mute to praise. "I like not only to be loved, but to be told that I am loved;" George Eliot was not ashamed to admit, "the realm of silence is for the grave."

Therefore, if there is a friend you value, a loved one you hold dear, an associate you like, a person you admire, give him your praise, your recognition, your appreciation, your thoughtful understanding. No one has yet lost a friend, or caused his wife heartburn as a result of overstuffing them with praise. And if we are in the habit of giving credit to others, we will cultivate our hearts to think the beautiful thoughts which will in the end make us more appreciative and confident of ourselves.

WHAT DEATH CAN TEACH US ABOUT LIFE

We can be appreciative and grateful folk for such simple things as the gifts of life and of health (whatever we have of it) and for the cherished hours we can spend within our family circle. And as life can bring us living appreciation, death can endow us with human comprehension. Some experiences in life have a certain poignancy to convey a message. Death can teach us something about life. It taught me. From the dark clouds of sorrow, I extracted a silver lining of enthusiasm for life.

Tragedy and death know no boundaries and respect not youth. Their visitation upon us is always horror-ridden and repellent. But when the bloody, devastating paws of death pluck the very young and the very near and dear together—mother and child—we are touched and shaken to the foundation of our very being. We grind our teeth and murmur: Why, why, why?

Such a cup of agonizing bitterness was overflowing in my own community some time ago, when a young family was shattered by death's unexpected blow. The young mother with her three young was on the way home, after returning from a medical check-up, when her car collided with a truck. She died instantly behind the wheel, with the oldest of her children, four-year-old Michelle—inseparable and inordinately attached to her in life—joining her in death. Neither did her two other children make it home that day. The youngest, 11-month-old Lorie, was crushed to her bones and only miraculously survived. But her older sister, three-year-old Pamela, was still hovering between life and death, unconsciously struggling and gasping for breath.

And so, after returning from the fresh gravesite of his young wife and child, the anguished father now stood at the bedside of a child, left-over from death's wreckage. He whispered to his unconscious and coma-stricken little girl: "Daddy is here, Daddy is here." But the sweet little child didn't know it. Neither did she know why she was cast in that iron cage for intensive care. She only breathed and struggled. And the father, standing by, only prayed, by day and by night—waiting.

And suddenly the whole world was painfully squeezed into focus of just one sweet little child in her struggle for the right to live. And as it were, God Himself was put to task in the words of the Hebrew patriarch, "Will the Judge of all earth not do justice?"

You are revolted, you don't submit, you question. Why? And you are not really waiting for the answer because you know it will not come to satisfy your mortal reasoning and rationale. You must stand there eye-dazed and wait and pray and wait and pray, believing that where you can't understand, you must still have faith, and where you can't change, you must still accept, if you are to have something left over to you of the goodness of life.

Then you go home and treasure the life of your own life, your own dear ones—children and all. And you know and feel, as you never knew and felt before, that life is a gift, to be embraced and cherished. And that while it's short, it can be stretched, ennobled, in breadth and in depth, adding to it a determination to bring a keener awareness of its precious currency and value. And in your new-found revelation, you are determined to give to life's brevity a life-intensity and declare with George Bernard Shaw: "Life is no brief candle for me. It is a sort of splendid torch which I have got hold of for a moment and I want to make it burn as brightly as possible before handing it on to future generations."

And you are happy in life, for it's the gift of all gifts, and nothing seems as important as seeing your wife and your children alive and smiling and giving and taking, in laughter and in tears—but alive, live and real. And you are happy in time and say today is the day. Time is not enough. Time is too little for tomorrow. Tomorrow is in tomorrow's time and if you don't know the value of its preciousness today, why should you know any better the next day?

And then you come to understand, as you never understood before, that you are not alone in this world. And that your life is a part of the mainstream of the everlasting river of humanity, in whose sympathy you share and in whose sadness you partake and in whose joys you bathe. And knowing that there is enough misery abroad in the world, enough sorrow and death, enough pain and suffering—a common brotherhood of humanity—you suddenly want to change yourself and the whole world. You are determined in resolution that there is enough adversity and horror and pain menacing your brother, there is enough struggle and tribulation, there is enough disease and anguish—and enough is enough! Perhaps, perhaps you say, I can change this by spreading a little comfort and joy around me; by giving the generous gift to my fellowman; by shedding the brightness of warmth where darkness has been dimming—to give a little of myself to stand larger than myself, by living fully and gratefully, here and now, in myself and with others.

Human life is a struggle and an achievement, but it is also a gift. And this gift is as good as is the spirit in which we receive it. It is, therefore, for us the living to learn from the bitter lessons of death how precious the short span of life is: how life can be mutilated by putting it off, by compromising it, by embittering it.

Life is too short for hatred, malice, hurt and revenge. Too many are the enemies assaulting the individual human life to permit man himself to turn foe against himself, against his neighbor. We have a common brotherhood in misery, can't we have a common brotherhood in ecstasy as well?

For we are besieged by fears within us, imbedded in our

human nature; and fears outside us lurking in physical nature. We fear others and we fear ourselves; we fear living and we fear dying. We fear the ills of the body and of the mind, of the heart and of the soul.

We are frail and confounded. We pray to live a long life and yet hate the condition of the longer life that God grants us at old age. As we want to know and to understand more, we want to be appreciated and to be understood evermore. We have a common humanity; might we not gain a union of sympathy and solidarity among us? Might we not feel in our own agony the pain of others; in our own tribulations the struggles of others; in our own unfulfillment the need for compassion toward others?

Let us then turn our thoughts from malice and greed to loving kindness and humanity, that we may truly know that God's work is indeed our work and His love unites us all. There is enough glory and adventure, struggle and sublimity, to lift us in orbit as a chorus of angels in praise of our humanity—in clasping the hand of man in reaching out for the hand of God. Death is all around us (disease is bred within us in the unseen battalions of swarming virus) but so is life. And while we live, we can make the minutes of our life longer by sharing them with others in noble endeavor; the hours of our life more lasting by occupying ourselves with things of beauty and a truth higher than ourselves; the weeks of our life fuller by filling their contents with the fulfilling stuff that lifts the soul; the months, the years more enduring by crowning them with the eternal and indestructible heritage of the human spirit—thereby granting ourselves immortality by virtue of having contributed our share to the common good that can never die.

4.

ALL CREATION IS JOY

The everlasting song is still
unsung,
And the eternal tale is never
told:
Earth and the ancient joy are ever
young,
It is the heart that withers and
grows old.

—John Hall Wheelock

OF ALL LIVING THINGS ON EARTH, THE MOST MOODY
and temperamental creature is man. In ecstasy, he rises to
splendid self-expression; in tragedy, he plunges to self-
explosion. He is the only animal capable of both crying and
laughing. He can retreat within himself to drown in the
morbid pool of his own tears; or he can mingle with the
world to become enthralled by its intoxicating chalice of
dripping joys and enchantments.

The choice is ours. And we are given the sage and
friendly advice to be jubilant and optimistic: "Rejoice!"
Biblical literature is ablaze with the fiery and repeated
exhortations of the imperative to be joyous in disposition,
to rejoice in exultation. No wonder R. W. Dale expressed
this thought of contrition over gloom: "We ask God to
forgive us for our evil thoughts and evil temper, but rarely,
if ever, ask Him to forgive us for our sadness."

Excessive sadness and moodiness can indeed be a sinful

act inasmuch as it causes a distortion in our character and divine image. For in negative thinking and despairing remorse, we shrivel to a self-pitying preoccupation, to a mere shadow of our living personality. When we retreat in depression and crawl into a hole of lonely isolation, we cease growing. We stop mingling with the world and find ourselves entombed in black and brooding melancholy. The mind turns upon itself to confront a windowless cave, walled off to all vision and outside perspective, a psychic dead end of despair and life imprisonment.

Man's redeeming solace is in joy. "Joy is energy" and energy is joy. It's an outgoing quality of spiritual dynamism, a chemical ingredient of ethical fulfillment, both in one's self and in others.

Sadness is sinful because it causes self-absorption instead of self-expansion; partial suicide, instead of newly born aliveness. Tormenting anxiety and gloom can cripple a person's mind and snuff out the light of his soul. Such an individual will look for closed hiding places when he should be seeking open, blooming gardens where he can partake of the air of growth and of the sunshine of warming glorification.

Joy to man is not optional luxury. It's a vital prerequisite of life itself. "No child is born except through pleasure and joy," said the Besht. The doctrine of joy is ingrained in the noblest teachings of the great religions. Life must not be endured in self-abnegation but glorified and enjoyed. And when the joys of living and the cheerful delights of everyday life, in all their purity and nobility, become manifestations of the divine, what greater glory can there be to the Creator! For joy is more than the indulgence of the senses. It's more than the happiness of making money for money's sake, of pleasure for pleasure's sake, of power for power's sake. There must be a higher aim, a nobler purpose, the end of which is human fulfillment and self-expression.

For the greatest and most durable and ennobling joys of life are those rendered through meaningful self-fulfillment and self-expression. It is in the purifying and exhilarating experience in which we lose ourselves that we truly find ourselves.

In love as in creation, in music as in art, in friendship as in creative association, we derive the deepest joys when we lose ourselves in the subject that absorbs and transforms us. We grow in stature as we step out of ourselves to celebrate a world of blissful delights that infuses us with the universal joys of creation where everything joyfully sings praise unto God in the harmony of grace.

In joy we give nothing as much as ourselves. And it's in this giving that we are most enriched: in the joy of giving in love; in the joy of partaking in creation; in the joy of answering the inner yearnings of the spirit; in the joy of bringing the light of grace, beauty and truth in all the dark places; in the joy of our curious extension as we peer into the innermost world of the nucleus and the outermost twinkling worlds of the stars.

DOING IS JOY

Joy, not happiness, must be the ultimate in human life. For happiness is elusive and cannot always be guaranteed, whereas joy can be almost invariably created by us. At all times, we are capable of engaging in such activities that will bring us delightful sensations and the joys of living. We might simply begin by greeting each day with a positive approach and a joyous appreciation for life itself, agreeing with Seneca that, "When a man has said, 'I have lived,' every morning he arises he receives a bonus."

Joys, unlike happiness, come in the plural (there are no "happinesses") to indicate that they are by-products of many little acts and habits of grace that add up to a great and productive life.

Happiness and ease can come to all animal life. Elephants and cows are satisfied and contented in the fullness of their stomach. Human beings need fulfillment of soul as well. It was Mencken who graphically illustrated this point by shrewdly observing, "Happiness isn't everything: a hog is always happier than a man, and bacteria are always happier than hogs." Mr. Mencken's unceremonious lumping together of this trio—man, hog and bacteria—and the yardstick he uses for the measurements of the individual units of happiness apportioned to each, may remain enigmatic and baffling to us. One thing, however, is clear in his observation: Passive happiness and the ease of comfort aren't necessarily the ingredients of a great life. We do not reject happy living itself, but we reject happy living in itself alone as a goal of life without the creative and titillating qualities of the adventurous spirit which perceives that although, "Much we know . . . more we dream."

Every human being is master of a world of symbols and the fashioning powers of language and reason. All his wisdom and vision and joy come to him by acts of affirmation. He is witness and observer, judge and jury, and his stamp seals the verdict in the "court room" of his own life. It is there where he glimpses revelations, where he views visions and brings the relationship of all that he sees into a harmony "to become all things."

We recall the biblical description how, after the works of creation were completed, Adam was placed in his paradise to be given the supreme responsibility of giving names to all living things, "and whatsoever the man would call every living creature, that was to be its name," symbolizing the need for man to engage in meaningful affirmations and definitions in order to bring the reality of his experience into a world of life.

This is our destiny as masters in creation: doing is joy and knowing is fun, although it proves painful at times; the price is worth the man. Human fulfillment, the crown of creative joy, is the result of an optimistic and joyous affirmation of the worthiness of life, of the goodness of man and of the value of an inward spirit and a native ability to rejoice in ourselves—to have faith in our own power of thrust toward the stars.

For what is life? A dream, a doom; a joy, a jest; a smile, a sigh; a throb, a storm; a leaf blown in the wind; a spirit rooted in the Eternal Flame? Whatever we choose in our human vocabulary and experience, whatever eloquence and imagery we give to life, it creates the world of our reality.

We communicate by the power of eloquent affirmation. We inherit life by the strength of our vision, by our ability to be productive, by mingling and belonging—merging our individual lives with the life of humanity. Outgoing joy, then, not brooding retirement from life, is the key word in human expansion and growth. Because joy involves more than one individual and comes in the sharing of experiences with others, we belong when we are joyous; we are fulfilled in mirth; we are participants in an ode of joy that has its echoes in the roots of heaven.

OPEN A WINDOW TO THE WORLD—CREATE JOY!

For those tossed in a boisterous sea of troubles, there is apparently little room for optimism and good cheer. They may reject out of hand the precept of "Enjoy yourself," with an inverted pessimism of resignation: "It's later than you think."

It's too late, some will say. There is too little in their own life to cheer them. They are spending all their time and overtime to deal with the heartaches and hard pressing problems of the day. How can you find time for joy in life when there is so little in your life that you really like?

Create it! Every person is still master of his own soul. And what he is alone—in himself and by himself, what no one else can give him or take away from him—is still the most precious element in one's destiny. No one will deny that physical poverty, agonizing loneliness and shattering disease can make life miserable and joyless. But morbid self-absorption is of little help. On the contrary, it will accentuate the problem at hand by making it a festering and spreading sore. There is really very little choice for us. We can focus our attention and our life energies on ourselves by filling our minds with mirrors reflecting only our own little world of petty ambitions and fleeting pleasures; or we can merge ourselves with the mainstream of life by opening up our minds with windows that will extend into the great world of outgoing joy and enduring involvement.

A mature person is one who has learned to break out of himself—not away from himself—in order to bring a greater measure of meaning and richness into his individual life; who has mastered the art of integrating his personality by finding those satisfactions and joys in himself and in his work that will bring enjoyment and service to others; who can come to think of others before he considers his own comfort and pleasure. A mature person, in a word, is a self-extended individual.

People who are self-centered and self-obsessed always live

in a glaring world of the blinding mirrors of their own dazzling self-indulgence and super-sensitivity. They are imprisoned to an awkward and self-conscious existence by "taking their own pulse," imagining exaggerated problems, hurts and humiliation. The mental hypochondriac who can't get off his own hands imagines the whole world to focus on him, against him. He sees insult where there isn't; malice where there is none. He is in the way of himself, blocked in the dead end of his own body weight. So vain is he in his egocentricity that he causes his personality to be arrested in development, always to remain an immature infantile wrapped up in a bundle of his own sensations and clamoring complexities.

At all times and circumstances, in our happy moods as well as in our anguished moments, we can find relief by releasing ourselves from the narrow world of a "mirror mind," which can turn into a torture chamber of mental anguish for us. "Anxiety," one psychiatrist remarked, has the same root as the Latin word "angina," which means narrowness, a narrow pass. The egocentric, being hemmed in by some neurotic narrowness of personality and outlook, finds himself hopelessly caught in a squeeze of his own making until he can hear Balaam's proverbial ass speaking for his better self in chastisement: "What have I done unto thee that you have struck me these three times?"

Men and women who feel inadequate, unfulfilled and troubled by some weakness, handicap or unsmiling fortune, can always find compensating interests and stimulations outside themselves that will bring them a measure of joy and satisfaction in life. Instead of treading their own narrow path of crushing pressure and resounding regret "What have I done . . . ?" they might better face the greater arena of a world larger than themselves and by affirming it, find enough love and grace, laughter and joy to make living challenging and worthwhile.

INVEST YOUR LIFE IN SOMETHING WORTHWHILE

A restful soul in perpetual ease is like restful water in a stationary tub, always in danger of becoming stagnant and rustful.

John Burroughs articulated this truth when he concluded that, "An idle man is a wretched man." Idleness is festering scum and death. And if life has any comprehensible meaning to us at all, it is in the saving grace that is to be found in our daily tasks and responsibilities that lie immediately at hand, which alone can redeem us from our own ferocious explosiveness.

Observe life and you'll find its immediate purpose and fulfillment. What is that end of life? It is, as best as we know, to dignify the means by which we live and to add beauty and nobility to our name that will be added to the guest list of lodgers on this planet. And since we are not owners and perpetual masters of our earth, we must pay for our ticket with saving toil so as to enjoy every sweet movement of our ride on God's global merry-go-round.

We must constantly be on the move. We must have something to do. We must have some challenge, some work, some cause in which we can invest our creative energies. We must, for our own safety and security, invest ourselves in a love, in an ideal, in a project that will transcend us and redeem us.

Every person, by reason of intelligence and potential power, is a danger to himself. There is enough flammable material and latent energy within us to make us explode like

fire crackers that go up in fury and smoke. The wise coun-
selor pleads for self-expression, not self-explosion. The power
that is in us must be harnessed constructively or it will be
wasted; worse yet, it will bring us to personal disintegration
and individual injury.

The pattern of growthful fulfillment is unique: life is
on the move. The birds build their nests in the trees, the
trees blow into bloom in the sun and man grows as he
moves in creation and among men.

If you would crave for a life that will hold its savor to
its very end; if you would pray for living never to become
empty and stagnant and rusting; if you would join the army
of watchers of sunny skies, the listeners of thrilling laughter,
the gazers of beauty in distant hills—then, by all means,
invest your life by being on the go.

The imprisoned soul needs the freedom of the whole
world, not the tinkering with one's self, the preoccupation
with one life, no matter how unique that life may be. In
the surrender of the fulfilled self toward an extension in a
greater world of living and experiencing, we become the
electric poles that will carry light to that open and bright
city which is the City of God. Because when we shoulder
a burden and move from a selfish preoccupation to a selfless
interest, we objectify our individual life and transmute it
to a total life of self-extension and self-enlargement.

W. Beran Wolfe taught the ghostly malcontents of his
day that by absorbing themselves only in their own interests
and desires they have failed to derive the deeper joys that
are inherent in human relations and involvement, thus creating their own misery and unhappiness. He wisely noted
that human fulfillment is not to be sought "as if it were a
pot of gold at the end of a rainbow, but among human
beings, who are living richly and fully the good life. If

you observe a really happy man you will find him building a boat, writing a symphony, educating his son, growing dahlias in his garden . . . living 24 crowded hours of the day."

And if we have none of these life-absorbing, life-sustaining hobbies, we can still earn our life by leaving "no tender word unsaid," no sweet melody unheeded, no beautiful sight unglimpsed. Keep moving, we must!

THE JOY IN GIVING

There is an abiding and profound moral truth in the nature of two not too distant seas—the Sea of Galilee and the Dead Sea. Both are nurtured by the headwaters of the Jordan. But while their source of life springs from the same fountainhead, they remain intrinsically different in the husbandry of their fluid gift.

The Sea of Galilee gives out a drop of its living waters for every drop it receives. Because there is a balanced measure of incoming and outgoing waves, it always remains a new sea with fresh vitality—a living world with life teeming within and leaf fluttering without. Not so is the Dead Sea. For every liquid drop it receives, it gives nothing in return. Because it is always at the receiving end, never to be moved by the generous impulse of giving, it's a stagnant sea, with torpid sluggishness—a dead sea harboring nothing but salty deposits that banish life from its midst.

Like those two seas, the lives of men are determined not by their capacity to receive but by their ability to give—to give of themselves in open and outgoing relationships.

The stream that keeps moving will not stagnate; the life that keeps circulating will stay clean of physical and mental ills. The currents of life's stream must be kept going and flowing, inwardly and outwardly, in a perpetual ebb and flow, give and take. "Keep the currents moving," enjoins the wise John Burroughs. "Don't let your life stagnate."

Too many seek joy by focusing all their attention upon themselves. They fail because they dance in circles after their own tail, finding their chase to be elusive, their end a mirage. Why? Can it be that instead of moving forward and onward in open and clear outlets, they end up trotting in U-turns, always trapped in muddled waters of keeping themselves on their hands?

For no matter who we are and what we do, we can never be content with ourselves when we are contained within ourselves. We must seek some objective truth, some ethical possibility, some moral beauty, to keep life's stream from becoming a Dead Sea of stagnation, boredom and despair. Hear the voice of one of humanity's better children and gain the insight of the master's truth: "It is only well with me when I have a chisel in my hand," said Michelangelo.

How does a person keep well and moving? Michelangelo found his answer in his chisel that became to him a personal expression of beauty and truth. The immortal visions of the man were etched in stone, becoming at once the master's self-extension. And like Michelangelo, each and everyone of us must find his particular "chisel," the tools by which he can carve out for himself such visions of beauty and nobility as to make his life coherently clear and outgoing with unitive purpose.

Get off your own hands, wisdom pleads with us, by escaping your mental ghetto. Invest your energies in exercises, from the simplest to the most sublime: in the energizing use of muscle and sweet labor; in the lusty engagement of mental attunement and emotional tone; in strolling in the fields for fresh air; in taking revitalizing walks in the

City of God for revealing glimpses. Get on, for God's sake! Move forward for your salvation. Every cathedral is built of many scattered stones and every destiny is structured by the many acts and habits of life. It is up to us to seek the tools for our inner construction, and the material wherewith we can fashion the mansion of our soul.

The "chisel," the instrument of objective truth, can save life from wretched morbidity and mold it into sublimity. And the most blissful and joyous lives are those that have found the answer to getting off their own hands and their self-attending petty interests and concerns as they become interfused with the mightier ongoing stream of life's refreshing waters.

The psychiatrist discovered this therapeutic truth in his insightful probings, while Walt Whitman said as much in his sparing poetic glimpses:

> I celebrate myself, and sing myself,
> And what I assume you shall assume,
> For every atom belonging to me as good
>   belongs to you.

THE SIMPLE JOYS OF LIVING

A stream that isn't in motion and remains cut off from the main, becomes at best only a muddled puddle, mirroring nothing else but outside reflections and sights.

Men and women who are cut off from the mainstream of life and live for themselves, end up enjoying little in themselves. They lose originality and languish in a fixed inertia of thinking and living that reflects nothing but outside impressions. They are the wretched whom Oscar Wilde scorns because they must live each other's lives and not their own.

The joyful and creative life must possess a living simplicity—original as far as possible, unadulterated as far as
obtainable—as its end.

Diogenes, the Greek philosopher, taught his contemporaries that the virtuous life is the simple life. And when
the simplicity-minded philosopher was asked by Alexander
the Great what he might do for him, Diogenes plainly replied, "Only step out of my sunlight." Then, Diogenes threw
away his only utensil, a simple shell from which he drank,
as he saw a boy drinking from his own hands. By doing so,
he didn't merely show defiance at civilized convenience. His
purpose was to demonstrate an exercise in the worthiness of
simple living as a virtue of humanity. And when he lustily
quenched his thirst by drinking from that cupful, formed
by his own ten fingers, he declared with childish exuberance
and innocence, "A child has beaten me in simplicity of living."

Here the ancient sage rejected a crude form of sophistication to remind himself of the simple joys of plain living and
the thrills of self-celebration with all its attendant delights
that are within reach at all times. Joyful living requires not
the wealth of a millionaire nor the luxury of a yacht, but
the richness of soul and the elegance of awareness. Drink,
Diogenes exhorts his contemporaries, from the cup of life,
with your own hands. Savor the living waters of natural
and childish innocence by marveling in your own capacity
to make life, to celebrate yourself, to reject luxury for its
own sake and things as the only vehicles of delight.

Many lives are muddled because they are fixed and
trapped within their own confines. They show nothing of
original motion, no sign of creative living. They only reflect
that which is projected upon their surface. They show shallow imitations of other lives. They either live in the yester-
days of wine and roses, or in the foggy dreams of tomorrow,

of some kind of a "Somewhere over the rainbow." In the meantime they forget that life cannot be put off; that they cannot live by postponement, toward a misty and dreamy tomorrow that may never come; that in order to have the slightest hope that "Man has Forever" they must not let the moment slip by unadorned. Because whatever roots we may have in eternity must take hold now.

If life is really so weak that it fails to move some people from their boring existence, it's only because it had become trapped in the muddy and slimy lagoon of self-containment. "It takes life to love Life," suggests Edgar Lee Masters. But when the stream has stagnated, the only life within it is a number of filthy, creeping, spineless little creatures that breed nothing but disease and muck. And what's true of liquid fluid, is true of the human mind.

A moving simplicity, and as far as possible an innate originality, is the crowning grace of a joyous and creative life: an awareness in things that happen, not an obsession in things that are bought; in clocks that strike time for holidays, not in relentless wrist-watches that push the blood pressure up to boiling; in enjoying a nice life, not in wrestling for rich living. To put it simply and aptly, in the words of William Henry Channing: "To live content with small means; to seek elegance rather than luxury, and refinement rather than fashion; to be worthy . . . to study hard, think quietly, talk gently, act frankly; to listen to the stars and birds, to babes and sages, with open heart; to bear all cheerfully, do all bravely, await occasions, hurry never; in a word, to let the spiritual, unbidden and unconscious, grow up through the common."

5.

LIFE IS NOT ALL PLEASURE

Out of the earth, the rose,
Out of the night, the dawn:
Out of my heart, with all its woes,
High courage to press on.

—Laura Lee Randall

MATURITY OF WISDOM AND YEARS TEACHES US THAT LIFE
is not all pleasure, living is not all a garden of Eden and
we can't always be victors in life, snatching laurels and
gaining medals. Even the heavenly ladder in Jacob's dream,
linking the animal kingdom with the divine kingdom, is a
vision of reality, of ups and downs, of God's angels ascending and descending in both directions.

We all have our ups and downs. Under the most ideal
circumstances we come face to face with reality that all
things in life are composed of "mighty opposites"—sunrise
and sunset, flow and ebb, joy and sorrow, triumph and
tragedy, victory and defeat, life and death. We cannot accept
the sweet and reject the bitter if we are to find a measure
of equanimity and serene composure in climbing life's mountain and in proclaiming at the end of the trying journey:
"I have reached the summit and behold I see a new horizon."
To some of us the rocky path seems obstructed and insur-
mountable. Rocks to the mountaineer can be stumbling
stones or stepping stones, and so it is with life. For those

who look up, the journey is always worth the effort, the uphill climb.

We can face failure, sorrow, defeat, with rebellion, scorn and cynicism, as our cup of bitterness overflows not only in what we have lost but also in what we have left. Or we can mobilize our faith, courage and hope in accepting what cannot be changed, the inevitable that must be faced, and make the most of our predicament. By doing so we can snatch the honey of reconciliation from the jaws of defeat.

There are the despondent losers who wallow in the salty tears of self-pity and self-hate; who bruised and disgruntled, set out to roar an outcry of fury and disbelief. The shaken foundations of their own world give rise to a curl of the lip and a sneer of protest. They rail against God, man and the goodness of life. In bitter frustration they bewail the calamity of their heartless circumstances and question with tortured heart: "Is there a plan within the universe, or any pattern in human life? Is it by law or accident we live, by will or chance we end our span of strife? How can we justify the ways of God, and prove that pain is destined for our good, declare each suffering life a perfect whole, pronounce each doubt a purpose understood?"

We cannot give answers to all questions. But we are given a life on this earth. Why? We cannot tell. How? We do not know. And all we are asked in return for this life is to give it meaning as best as we can without pretending to know all the answers; for alas, we don't even possess the wisdom to ask all the pertinent questions related to our cosmic being. We know that our birth is conceived in darkness and must not be lost in a forgetfulness of a dead end of oblivion. Anguish, pain, suffering, sorrow, far from being alienating forces to envenom our beings, can become stepping stones to a perceptive ascent of sensitivity, human sympathy and self-revelation.

TO RISE ABOVE DEFEAT

Greatness is a measure of one's ability to rise above defeat: to stand up against the blows with which nature afflicts us mortals, and if possible to transform weakness into strength, humiliation into humility, failure into fortitude. Agonizing deafness that shut the gates of sound with seemingly tragic consequences to the genius of musical sound, Beethoven, opened up new vistas of inner sound to the author of the heaven-soaring "Ode of Joy." Some of the world's greatest personalities and careers have emerged from disabling handicaps. Homer was blind; Milton, deaf; Rembrandt, troubled; Alexander Pope, a hunchback; Edgar Allen Poe, a psycho-neurotic; Charles Darwin, an invalid; Julius Caesar, an epileptic; Franklin D. Roosevelt, a polio victim; John F. Kennedy, racked with pain; Richard M. Nixon, a defeated politician.

These remarkable people didn't allow handicaps, deficiencies and disappointments to divert them from their higher goals of life. Neither did they brood in self-pity and rebellion to ruin the foundations of their creative processes. When their outer coil of physical and mental fitness was flawed, they delved into their inner resources with deepening strength and sharpened perceptiveness, giving vent to their talents and inward spirit. After facing crushing defeat, which would have humbled ordinary people, they rose in adventurous daring to accept their bundles of trouble and pain only to give rise to compensating qualities of powerful self-expression and self-fulfillment. They gave true meaning to the words of Goethe:

> Who never ate his bread in sorrow,
> Who never spent the darksome hours,
> Weeping, and waiting for the morrow,
> He knows ye not, ye heavenly Powers.

Most of us would be content to live a life of humble means and small adventures, sparing ourselves of the bitter "bread of sorrow" and the tears of "darksome hours." We would also gladly forgo the rewarding compensations that come with the self-revelation of knowing the "heavenly Powers." But since pain to most of us comes as an uninvited guest and sorrow (to all of us) as an unwanted boarder, we might as well accept our lot with the sweet resignation that will allow us to mellow in the refinery of experience and to be tempered in the universal brotherhood of man's most common destiny—struggle. Thus, we may become more sensitive and sympathetic to the hurts of others in pain and in sorrow and hear the sweet sad music of humanity.

THE TWIN BROTHERHOOD OF AGONY AND ECSTASY

Even in our ecstasy, we cannot escape agony. Both are necessary and unavoidable components of life. As yeast gives rise to dough, so does trial add depth and solemnity to life. The experiences of pain, of endurance, of perseverance are as much spices of life as pleasure itself. They make the man. Nothing worthwhile is created without trouble, effort and tears.

Our birth, our living and our loving are conceived in longing and travail. Everything that sings cries; the whole universe is a chorus of voices; creation prays, sighs, sings and longs. Life, like a Jacob's ladder stretching heavenward, with ups and downs, is playing its game with the human mass. The entire range of man's existence is marked by perpetual motion (motion and not inertia): a curious will to embark upon the newest venture, to discover the farthest horizon, to break the latest record, to meet the gravest challenge.

Motion, the source of all universal power and balance is the lifeline of man's living. By feeding on it he is revitalized and reenergized. Motion implies friction; hence the rubbing pain, the bumpy jerks, the unavoidable wreckages sadly littering the highways and byways of life.

If this is nothing but a merry-go-round viciously turning about and always returning to its point of departure—who cares! We haven't made the rules of the game. We are only given a ticket for the ride. Why fret and complain? It can be a charming trip if we can but see the exciting colors of life passing our way and the gay music of humanity rushing toward us. Our fortunes lie not in remote stars of cold calculation and equation; nor are our visions born of proven certainties, but in our inward soul: in human comprehension, in feelingful extension and in a relatedness of identification. And while going round and round, we can assume the fortitude of faith in the Benevolent Conductor of our Amazement Park, who at will makes the wheels turn in cycles and the stars spin in motion.

Life is not an aimless evanescence. Man's vision is limited. He saw a flat world and proved wrong in his science, but later he saw heaven and moved upward—like on a Jacob's ladder—treading with the angels in space. Is this merry-go-round of life a child's play, motion without direction, a hide-and-seek game emerging from the shadows of nowhere to glide into the darkness of nowhere? Not so to the believer. (And all men who see believe.)

There is orderliness, relatedness, beauty and meaning in this world of ours, a speck in an ocean of eternity of countless worlds. A Universal purpose permeates all. Only the fool will call it colossal accident, cosmic blunder and blind purposelessness. If life be a merry-go-round, it can be joyous and exciting. Better a merry-go-round than a misery-go-round. And much depends upon our faith and outlook on life.

Unfortunately few are those who have mastered the ultimate art of life in being able to roll with the bumps. Some among us who have been unduly afflicted with maladies and tribulations groan in protest and wallow in tears. Like Job of old they are embittered by the chalice of life that has been apportioned to them. And since pain and agony are the most potent individualizers, they often claim that they have been unjustly singled out as targets of the "slings and arrows of outrageous fortune."

The truth is that very few residents of this planet are free from vexation and pain. Most of us wouldn't exchange places with some bright and smiling faces we see, after we have discovered what ails them. Were we to peek into our neighbor's soul, we might prefer our own bundle of toil and tribulation.

Our life and what we do with it is clearly the mirror of our own soul. If we assume a cheerful disposition and an optimistic view, we may come to follow the simple wisdom of the writer who counsels us to remember that the tea-kettle sings even though it is up to its neck in hot water. Does singing necessarily reduce the heat, the pain? Probably not. But it certainly reduces the black-tarred isolating wall of melancholy, bitterness and loneliness.

YOU ARE NOT ALONE IN YOUR ANGUISH

Do you experience hardship or pain? You are not alone in your anguish. Millions of others, at one time or another, are in the same brotherhood of misery. What comfort is it to you when it is your heart that aches, your body that is stung? Perhaps very little. But the choices are few and the freedom is yours to choose: (in spite of everything) sing if you can, cry if you must—hope in either case. "God sometimes puts us on our back so that we may look upward."

At times it may take a lot of courage to look upward: countless tears, much sweat and an immeasurable sense of endurance and perseverance. But our real choice, we are told repeatedly, is not in having the kind of life we love but in loving the kind of life we have by making the most of it, with all the beauty and grace that we can add to it.

For our human beauty far surpasses our frail misery. This point is boldly made in the following anecdote. It is related that the great French master Renoir was afflicted with incurable rheumatism that grew worse with the passage of time. So severe was his affliction toward the end that whenever he painted he was placed in a chair to support his flabby muscle and faltering grip. And when he applied the paint brush his pain was so intense that perspiration drenched his body and agony seized his soul. "Why torture yourself to do more?" pleaded one of his disciples as he saw the artist struggling to finish his masterpiece. Renoir stopped for a moment as he gazed fondly at his favorite canvas. Then, like a sharp beam piercing through a cloud of darkness, a happy smile animated his pale face as he whispered softly: "The pain passes, but the beauty remains."

The insight and truth of the artist had taught Renoir that one's usefulness in the creation of beauty has everlasting value and helps man discover an optimism of living—in spite of trouble and affliction. It gives him the added strength of pulling himself up by his own bootstraps and thereby making life worthwhile, endurable and even excitable.

These, then, are the most faithful and reliable verities of life: beauty, truth and service. Through them our lives become transfixed and attain permanence in God's order of things.

Our lives are transformed through the beauty we see in things, through the service we give to things (and to each other) and through the truth we discover in our search for these noble qualities. And when we find them, the pain of wrestling with the forces of fate passes. Glory and struggle, agony and ecstasy are intermingled. We, then, do not live our lives in vain, even while we may live in pain. We fight as giants and triumph as gods for "the beauty remains."

But what is beauty? Ask the poets and the philosophers and masters of old. And they all agree that beauty is to the beholder. There is nothing in beauty until you discover it.

To the poet beauty is in song and words, to the painter it is in brush and color, to the composer it is in tonality and harmony, to the mathematician it is in computation and digits, to the scientist it is in the test tube and scientific discovery, to the farmer it is in the rustle of golden corn in the field.

Yet, each and every one of us ordinary people—worker and clerk, housewife and executive—can find beauty in the things we have and in the things we do to give us enough satisfaction to ameliorate the pain that is inevitable in life by the beauty that remains. Nature is a revelation of God, not an evolution of a neurotic cosmic disorder. But before seeing this revelation, we must find the revelation in ourselves. And we can be a revelation to ourselves by using our powers aright, by discovering our usefulness in the search for beauty and truth; in our dedication to service—no matter how frail and insignificant our contribution may be—by doing our share for the sum total of this generation. For as long as "the beauty remains" will not our pain be less consequential and poignant?

The search for beauty and truth can transform our lives

and transcend our daily tribulations. For beauty is a power, a relationship, a dialogue. It is never a passive happening. Speak to it and it will speak to you. Believe in it and it will live in you. Unite with it, breathe with it, bathe in it. For it is all part of life and you can become part of all that life—splendidly enlarged and transformed in simple purity.

The object lesson is plain: keep your head above water; endure and prevail. Live and mingle with the splendors you see.

Have you experienced failure? Have you been crushed by defeat? Have you been unappreciated? Have the bumps been wounding and the ascent perilous? Don't give up. Keep on trying. Often, failure is a prelude to success, defeat is a stepping stone to achievement. Today's shattered dream can be tomorrow's sperm of fulfillment.

Tomorrow is another day—another chance for a new start, a fresh beginning. Real conscious life begins with its awareness of self and ends with the oblivion of selfhood.

Every day's awakening is a test of life's self-endurance and self-consciousness. This, in essence, is the challenge of human life and intelligence—the ability to merge ourselves with the splendors that surround us, in spite of ourselves. We have a right to probe into the ultimate purpose of our life on earth; moreover, we have the intelligence to do so.

We are superior to the stars. Is this empty bragging, vainglory? No. Think of it, we know of the stars. The stars do not know of us. We do not endure in time as celestial "non-entities" but endure in soul, in life and consciousness. Herein lies our glory: in self-revelation and self-realization.

SUCCESS IS IN TRYING

We do not always glow in success. Success is never a straight ladder reaching upward. The reality of human achievement is closer to Amos B. Alcott's truth: "We mount to heaven mostly on the ruins of our cherished schemes, finding our failures were successes." But even if we are convinced that the blows of defeat are real and hurting, they must not necessarily be final and paralytical.

A writer once catalogued Abraham Lincoln's adverses, and they were many. He ran for the Legislature in Illinois and was badly swamped. He engaged in business, failed, and spent 17 years of his life to pay the debts of a worthless partner. He fell in love with a beautiful young lady to whom he became engaged, but she later died. He married a woman who was a constant drag and burden to him. Upon entering politics again, he was badly defeated for Congress. He failed to get an appointment to the U. S. Land Office. He failed dismally in his bid for the U. S. Senate. In 1856 he became a candidate for the vice presidency and was defeated. In 1858 he was defeated again by Douglas.

The crossroads of destiny and of men are mysterious. Were Lincoln to succeed in his business enterprise or in any other of the local offices that he pursued, would he not have lived a quiet successful life as a businessman or politician, coming at last to rest somewhere in a local cemetery, nameless to the world and unknown to generations? And would not the course of history of the United States and the world be far different today?

No one can tell for sure. One thing is certain. The star of Lincoln the man didn't shoot up straight in a glowing heaven. He never failed to dare even if it meant daring to fail. And he knew that one doesn't go without the other. In his stately biblical eloquence he would have probably paraphrased Josh Billings' aphorism, agreeing with its contents that "It ain't no disgrace for a man to fall; but to lay there and grunt, is."

Wasn't this Moon-Age of ours conceived in the travail

of challenge and national distress? We still remember how in May 25, 1961—when a depressed nation was brooding over the Bay of Pigs fiasco and Russia was supreme master in outer space—President John F. Kennedy, "in a mood to run harder," spoke the words that eventually took man to another world, outside his own. "I believe we should go to the moon," he said.

And out of hard-pressing challenges, temporary defeats and humiliating beginnings, the new age was ushered in, the age of the most significant "one giant leap for mankind."

Perhaps one of the follies of our time is the equation of convenience and ease, with conscience and grace. Modern life has been made so relatively easy and comfortable for many of us that we are often tempted to avoid pain at all cost, to detour suffering and to by-pass grief. Well, if the day ever comes, when we fully succeed in our shortcutting, all human experience will become computerized and pilled to death, turning half-human and half-chemical formula. Man must never die for lack of a pill but neither must he live to depend on it as a mental crutch. Human experience —joy as well as travail, intensive living and even tension —makes for extensive life.

It is generally believed that Mendelssohn's musical genius did not attain its fullest height and deepest fulfillment only because in his unruffled, easy and happy life he never came to grapple with the thunderous bolts of heaven, which while zigzagging a man's path in crushing force, in the clash of dark clouds, are capable at the same time of producing the brightest sights of a heaven, blazing in revelation and illumination.

Mendelssohn with all his gifts of lyrical expression, effortless beauty and poetic elegance, seldom scaled the heights of Beethoven, Brahms and Bach, who had experienced the terrible purgative powers of either loneliness and defeat, or the ecstasies of religious brooding. He came close to joining the company of the elect but he never quite made it. For his life lacked the cathartic experiences to hear with the soul instead of the ear, the sad and solemn music of humanity, as was the tragic circumstance of Beethoven. Mendelssohn's ingratiating music, while sweet and pleasant, has no profundity of thought, emotionalism of depth and vastness of dimension. His music is the story of his life: beautiful and serene but never seducing, transfixing and overwhelming. Because he was never compelled to cry in life, he was never impelled to ruminate from depth. He never paid the price of sublimity: never knowing ordeal and struggle, he failed to grope and invoke the heaven-stirring expressions of triumph over them.

A terrible commentary, but true nonetheless! Life's deeper joys and creative powers usually exact a toll in terms of pain, effort and sacrifice. Many people are at their best under duress and pressure. The days of drudgery and toil are made meaningful because they prepare us for the Sabbath Day of Rest. Without toil, rest would be a meaningless retirement. Without darkness, light would be a dazzling nuisance. Without ailing pain, healing power would lose its soothing comforts. The opposites not only attract in life but also make life attractive and measurable. And triumph is the child of endurance and perseverance—painstaking preparations, toil and tears.

Therefore, if the shadows of duress and pain, upheaval and pressure close in upon you, don't despair. The staying powers of bearing in patience and prevailing in solitude— true signs of maturity—will enable you to find the light of hope in the midst of the chaos of trauma, the sublimity of faith in the midst of heartless cynicism, the healing comfort in the midst of aching pain.

Blessed are the patient who wait and endure and persevere; for they shall know the true meaning of one poet's effervescent beauties: "These things are beautiful beyond belief: The pleasant weakness that comes after pain, the radiant greenness that comes after rain, the deepened faith that follows after grief, and the awakening to love again."

High intensity can produce high voltage of human energy and creativity. Dean Stanley tells the story of a German baron who built a huge Aeolian harp by stretching its wires from tower to tower in his castle. In summer days, the harp hardly emitted a sound. Still it hung in soundless repose. Then when autumn came and gentle breezes began to stir the strings, faint whispers of song began to permeate the air. But at last, when stormy winds swept over the castle and shook the musical strings, majestic sounds poured forth in trembling ecstasy. Tempestuous storm mingled with sublime sound. "Such a harp," concludes Mr. Stanley, "is the human heart. It does not yield its noblest music in the summer days of joy, but in the winter of trial. The sweetest songs on earth have been sung in sorrow. The richest things in character have been reached in pain."

LIVE YOUR AGE IN YOUR OWN TIME

Every life has its seasons, every age its compensations. There are things we can do well at 20 while others we do better at 40 and best at 60; and vice versa. Life gives us many options and possibilities. It is up to us to match the various stages of our life with the proper moods of temperament and dispositions of fitness so as to derive the maximum benefits of meaningful and joyful living. Life's gifts of adaptability should enable us to use to the utmost our best talents and powers at the height of their perspective peaks.

Clearly, there are definite advantages to every age. The

spring of youth and the summer of prime abound with the succulent and throbbing raw materials of life, bubbling with a fresh and vigorous exuberance; but they suffer from a lack of perspective and the mature wisdom and serenity that come with the sober gaze into the backyard of years and from the height and depth of ennobling experience and self-scrutiny.

The autumn of later years and the winter of colder nights, on the other hand, may suffer from waning physical vitality and slackening step and diminishing eyesight and ear sound —but not from dimming vision, failing perceptiveness and a dearth of vitality in a self-revealing life awareness and sobriety.

The simple pleasures that are never glimpsed during youth may come to us (if we do not submerge in self-pity) at a riper age. The very exercise of self, the unceremonious delight of living: of breathing and filling our lungs with living air, our hearts with the fresh blood of life and our minds with the reflective thoughts of worlds (a wonder of wonders)—these are experiences we come to relish in an awareness that comes to us from the perspective and sobriety of later years.

In an age when youth is a supreme virtue and status, at a time when the hairbrush goes hand in hand with the toothbrush and the hair color with the shoe color and the wig with face lifting, and the cosmetics with men, women and children (and over 30 is an age desperately to be avoided), it might be well to remember that age is what we do with it more than what it does to us. For regardless of the age we are in, the most boring and unwanted and unappreciated age is always the "now."

I remember the story of a little kitten that was once, after a long summer drought, sitting at the edge of a water trough when a light drizzle of rain began to fall. The little feline caught with its paw every drop of water as it came down the drainpipe, quenching its life-thirsting body.

If we, like that little kitten, can learn to catch, with human patience and trust, every drop of life as it comes our way, and appreciate its true value—at all ages and stages of life —we may better be able to live a life of noble means, with cheerful disposition and graceful serenity to the very end.

6.

THE CONQUEST OF INNER SPACE

The world is a looking glass and gives back to every man the reflection of his own face.
                                                            —William Makepeace Thackeray

ALL OF US, AT ONE TIME OR ANOTHER, FEEL A SENSE OF inadequacy and crave for added strength and superior powers. And the word that comes most readily to mind in connection with this understandable craving is that common, all-encompassing attribute: personality. In popular terms the word "personality" is used as if it were a special entity and endowment quite separate from the person. You thus hear people say: "What a wonderful personality he has," or "Here is a girl with a lot of personality," as if this was a cluster of pearls and jewels one wears externally.

In truth, however, personality is not something you can put on and off. It is neither a mask one wears (although the word itself is derived from the Latin "persona," which is an actor's mask), nor an ornament attached for decoration. It is more what a person is inside himself—alone in the dark as one shrewdly put it—in his bare soul and bones. The substance of personality is more real than putting on a smile, wearing a face and acting out the actor's lines—playing the role well for external appearance and applause. Indeed, it goes much deeper.

And don't confuse, I beg you, character and personality with image and popularity. The first is always the inner man of a person; the second is sometimes transparent, with a superficiality less than skin deep—the result of some kind of an externally caked makeup mud.

"Personality is not an elusive quality which radiates from certain fortunate persons and not from others," explain the noted psychologists S. Stansfeld Sargent and Kenneth Stafford. "It is unbelievably complex, the result of a lifetime of experiences and influences. Superficial changes, like affecting a genial smile, adopting a new hairdo, or cultivating poise, fail to affect our true personalities, which go deeper."

What is personality? In a word, the real you. You in inward living and action; you in secret praying and dreaming; you in personal action and reaction; you in thought and deed, feeling and emotion; you in relation to yourself, to your world, to your God—the total intangible psyche-complex of the mind's clearing house, giving currency to what makes you tick.

It is therefore unwise and certainly unscientific to classify people in generalities such as introverts or extroverts, subjective or objective. Facial features, bone structure and bodily attributes, once believed to be linked to personality characteristics, have been found to be prejudicial and misleading. The classic example of this myth is in Shakespeare's Julius Caesar, who casts suspicion on Cassius because of his lean and hungry look:

Let me have men about me that are fat;
Sleek-headed men, and such as sleep o'nights;
Yond Cassius has a lean and hungry look;
He thinks too much; such men are dangerous.

But this is fiction. A man's personality is not measured in size of skull, in shape of nose and in outward exterior impressions. Personality is the inward character of man. People are people with unique individualistic substance and depth, with personalities as distinct and as variable as their personalized fingerprints and vocal chords.

CHOOSING YOURSELF

What type of personality are you? Ask yourself and you are tempted to come up with some kind of classification. False. Personality measurement, scrutinizing yourself into the kind of person you are, is not like filling plasma bottles and labeling them as distinct blood types. In truth you are not the same person with the same personality all the time. You are a lot of people, a lot of times, in a lot of places. You are not constant and static. You change, you grow; you are shaping yourself, you are molding your character daily. You are constantly choosing yourself (or rejecting yourself?) as Kierkegaard in perceptual insight understood it.

In this sense a person is what he chooses, and choosing shapes his destiny and determines the kind of person he is, the sort of personality that makes him tick.

We might say that man, in his prime condition, is as much decision-maker as he is toolmaker. Choosing, then, becomes a human quality of the highest order. But choosing implies freedom. And, in spite of what they say or feel, some people are not quite free. They have no choice in being the kind of fulfilled persons they have a right of becoming, in making the best of themselves. They turn less human in their predicament and act like apes in a circus cage, dutifully awaiting their act of performance, but never quite free to act on their own, in their own natural element.

Such are the frustrated hollow persons, the shallow personalities whose symptoms show aggressiveness in action and awkwardness in reaction. They act tough and feel insecure. They give the appearance of importance and experience indignity. Because they know that theirs is only an act. They are not they, their own authentic selves. And it helps little to hurl a fist of rebellion at the steel bars of emotional and irrational encirclement.

Modern psychologists insist that emotional maturity—a basic condition for personality development—is an exercise of freedom. That is to say that no human being can truly come to develop his personality to the fullest in fulfilling his destiny, unless he is free to choose. The options for most of us may indeed be limited; nevertheless choice there must be.

And where there is choice there is chance. This is the message of the ancient prophets and herein lies the therapeutic balm of modern psychology: Don't wallow in guilt, in self-pity, in self-consciousness. Remember Micha's admonition to his people, "Shuva," Return! You still have a choice: Choose yourself, for you're a whole bundle of potentialities. Unwrap yourself freely. Find the gift of your original personality.

This concept of free will and human self-determination is a fundamental truth of religion. It is sound psychology as well. Human folly, blunder and bluster are not inhuman. They're only stupid. And stupidity is really no crime, considering that you have a choice to be stupid. The pity is only when stupidity is repeated again and again with the effects of eroding man's true personality and being.

THE FALL OF MAN OVER MOLEHILLS

How do most men fall? Not in climbing mountains but in stumbling over many little molehills. Man's erosion rarely starts with spectacular corruption and crime. It may begin with a puff, with an overindulgence, with an addiction, with the blotting out of the self-personality, with the effacing of the self-soul. And when the inner man is killed, everything else human is dead. The ape man takes over. And if that isn't a crime, what is?

Yet always, always, there is the opportunity of man for self-repair, for amends, for a return to himself—to choose his right and righteous self, his identity and fulfillment.

This is a noble concept and a human virtue—a divine endowment to give man a second chance—always the possibility to return, to make a move in the right direction, to make a new beginning, to discover new ethical possibilities.

For the prophetic utterance of "Shuva" in the original Hebrew is not the exact equivalent of repentance. Repentance has the stigma of sin, of condemnation mingled with toleration. Return is merely a correction in course, a refinement in orientation, in bearing. It breathes with the grace of charity, with forgiving and remembering that error is human, that blunder is not final. Man always has another chance.

The person who is relatively free from emotional guilt and self-deprecating anxieties is also free to choose himself and to shape his destiny freely, as far as humanly possible. He is free from undue guilt and since he has no struggle in justifying his existence and his usefulness as a mature human being, he has time to concentrate on the destiny of his becoming—the capacity for growth and fulfillment. He is happy with himself as he grows. Because growth is change and change robs boredom of its sting. He has no time for morbid self-martyrdom.

A choosing, a growing, a self-fulfilling person would seldom experience the anguish of L. Pearsall Smith's desperation that echoed the character of him who was threatened in the life of his soul: "What a bore it is, waking up in the morning always the same person."

For those who choose, there is a way out: change and growth in person and personality.

WE ALWAYS HAVE A SECOND CHANCE

How does a person change? How does one turn a new leaf to escape the hideous boredom of waking up in a dreamless mood, in yesterday's faded image?

Not by energy and motion alone. A thunderbolt is the wasted energy of clashing dark clouds. A revolving door is motion without direction. A person's energy must be channeled, well thought out and directed. It requires the wisdom to face reality, to accept change and to have the courage to admit error and benefit by it.

But alas, those who "change their skies but not themselves, who cross the seven seas," may virtually travel great distances and still go nowhere. They are, in reality, running away. We all know such people, to whom motion—motion without direction—has assumed a momentum of its own, a meaningless velocity of no real purpose. Why, then are they running? Why will a millionaire kill himself for another million? Why will a young disillusioned person commit suicide when life has to offer him so many other chances for personal enrichment? It is only because they have lost themselves: they have lost the capacity to lose and still recover; they have lost the personal elasticity to submit to change and surrender to other, perhaps richer, alternatives and possibilities.

Such people are terribly afraid, mostly of themselves. They abhor the thought of looking at themselves psychologically, eyeball to eyeball. They fear the emotional and spiritual emptiness they might discover. For when they stop to take stock of their coming and going—their running in all directions—they dismally discover that all their fearsome energy and activity has been to no visible purpose and end, only to cover up for an inner emptiness, to compensate for their emotional unfulfillment—a hollow clash of the dark clouds in their mental horizon.

For whatever they possess in personal wealth and worldly attainments, they actually don't have in experience. They may own an earthly kingdom and fail in having their inward kingdom of heaven. For their toil is only directed toward building the foundation of their own faltering ego. They always appear selfish, lonely and insecure. They cannot forgive themselves; nor others. A mistake to them is a scandal; a loss is total loss; for they are neither able nor willing to make the necessary adjustments by delving into their inner resources for self-recuperation, compassion and healing. They lack the personality resiliency that will allow them to "make do" with less than what they have been accustomed to; they fail in the comeback that will enable them to tap their hitherto ungiven selves—to save themselves, to fulfill themselves.

Perhaps much of the malaise of our time is due to modern man's dilemma of being swept by the mass energy of a computerized technological society with little initiative for individual freedom. If one must surrender his inward spiritual choice and abandon his freedom of individuality to mass patterns of social and organizational machines, can he feel more than a cog in a soulless generator?

What choice, then, is left for the modern individual who still hopes to preserve his individual character? The choice is still: choosing himself and unchoosing the patterns of mass identity to unfetter mechanical shackles.

"We must relearn to be alone," Henry King quotes Anne M. Lindbergh, and emphasizes the need of the individual to indulge in what seems to be a priceless and rare luxury today—"occasional total solitude."

Are you afraid that by being alone, you'll be lonely? Don't! "Being alone does not mean being lonely," he points out. "It means cutting off the external, the superficial and the superfluous, and seeking instead the inner strength which one finds best in solitude."

Are you afraid that by being alone you'll be a loner? Don't!

A walk alone at dusk, an early hour of solitude watching the dawn break, an idle interval on a garden bench, a short slow drive on back roads in beautiful country—no life is too busy for moments like these. . . . Everything pulls itself into perspective, often a better perspective. . . . We are at peace with ourselves.

". . . MAKE YOUR OWN ACQUAINTANCE"

In summary, Henry King suggests this simple and sound advice for a personal self-acquaintance: "Make it a point to stop and take time to make your own acquaintance. You'll probably get something of a surprise. Because you'll be meeting a very nice and stimulating person—yourself!"

Life presents us with untold opportunities of meeting ourselves head-on, for a self-acquaintance and man-to-heart dialogue. It is up to us to utilize them.

A crisis can often jolt us out of mulish apathy and rock our little boat of life from drifting aimlessly. The jolt may at the moment be unpleasant and rough to take, but it can spare us from capsizing in murky waters.

We are still captains of our souls and masters of our fate as long as we can exert some measure of direction and control over the cross-currents of life. A vacation, for instance, can be a happy opportunity to retreat from daily burdens and pressures; it might also give us a new look in handling ourselves and in evaluating our values. It can offer us pleasure as well as solace—a retreat from the organized frenzied mass as well as a refreshment of personality and soul.

But the ultimate test of life lies in our ability to meet every situation that comes our way by making the best of it. To be grateful for everything and surrender to change serenely is the supreme triumph of self-mastery.

An ancient Talmudic sage put it this way: Offer a blessing over adversity as you do over good fortune. For adversity, quite often, can bring us personal resolve and refinement. For if it brings us low, it gives us depth; if it singles us out adversely, it offers us solemnity; if it pains us, it brings us closer to ourselves. Emerson said as much in his own inimitable style, "When it is dark enough, men see the stars." And an Oriental proverb has it that, "All sunshine makes a desert."

Sometimes it takes a few dark spots to sharpen our focus for contrast and comparison, and to brighten our sense of appreciation. It takes a major crisis to put one on his knees, proverbially speaking, to make him think and reconstruct himself. Profound experiences, sickness or crisis, change a person for good or worse. It is up to us to accept adversity with a blessing on our lips and making the most of it, welcome it for its opportunity that it "introduces a man to himself."

The horizontal citizen in a hospital bed, who has joined the society of sufferers, has a choice in two directions. He can allow his sick body to percolate into boiling mental ills of self-pity and outer bitterness, cursing himself and his fate Job-like; or he can convert his illness into a blessing of sorts: to give him a clearer perspective, a sharper mental and spiritual awareness, an opportunity to change his person, enhance his personality and reap dividends out of his illness.

For crisis sensitizes a person. It permits him to feel the

real sensibilities of life—not luxuries—which come in the simplest acts of friendship and love. A friend's smile is a full heaven's sunshine; a get-well note is a world of solidarity; a graceful gesture—the smallest and usually nameless acts of kindness—assumes significance and heartfelt appreciation. Crisis personalizes a person. It gives him the requisite leisure to look upward, to raise his sights while he lies flat on his back. Responsibility melts while humility is heightened; pressure crumbles while perception grows. Suddenly, the things that always seemed so important and worth killing one's self for, diminish in their dimension and size. Values change, the person matures; suddenly he discovers the secret depths that come to him when he is alone, leaving the "squinting, sprinting and shoving world." He sees a new dimension in his life, a new awareness of gratitude, a second chance for recovery: a chance at his health, at his life, at himself.

"Even pain," says Dr. Louis E. Bisch, "confers spiritual insight, a beauty of outlook, a philosophy of life, and an understanding and forgiveness of humanity. . . ." Crisis and suffering have cleansing powers to make a person see the difference between superfluous luxury and living comprehension. It can bring a man down to himself and cut him down to the size of his normal and most perceptive life-yearnings.

HAPPINESS IS CHARACTER

It is a sad commentary on life, yet how true it is: some people really start living only after they have come face to face with the shadows of darkness and crisis. Suddenly, in the absence of the most elementary and simple amenities of a healthy and normal life, they come to appreciate the most precious gift of mortals—life itself. "For," as Dr. Bisch, in his rich personal experiences with patients once observed, "only when the way straitens and the gate grows narrow, do some people discover their soul, their God, or their life work."

A person may sometimes be required to assume those heroic qualities that compel him to gain the human comprehension that is opened up to him as "the gate grows narrow." The cultivation of character and personality will give us that added and needed dimension of humanity. For this is really what should matter to us more than anything else. Because what counts most in life is not the pleasure of external things but the pleasure of one's own company: the joy of what we can be to ourselves, the kind of inward harmony that we can discover in our inner recesses of conscience and self-fulfilling humanity. Henry Ward Beecher said it in enlightening brevity: "Happiness is not the end of life; character is."

The test is simple. Do you like yourself when you are alone in your own solitary company? Are you capable of meditation, introspection and self-dialogue? If not, look out—you're in trouble! You have failed to build up the cornerstone of your character and the ability to stand alone, on your own, to draw upon your inner resources. And since crisis is the isolating experience of finding one's self alone, in facing up to trouble—the test is crucial.

Perhaps this is where we moderns have failed: We have worked so hard at convenience that we have often neglected courage. We have stressed life insurance, above ever-living sureties; financial security, above self-trust; household comforts above home solace. We have put too much trust in production and mobility at the expense of character and nobility. Perhaps making a living is part of this rut-race;

but it should never hamper life itself. For the supreme challenge to the individual person is not to make living easier but to make life stronger: to build character and the personal resiliency to be able to face trouble and stand up to the onslaught of pain and defeat, as unavoidable spices of life.

We need courage, plenty of it, to face life. And life is a process of giving and taking, losing and regaining. And unless we build up our character and make weakness and failure work for us to recoup whatever losses we have, we will find ourselves grounded and despondent. This quality of bouncing back, of picking up our personal leftovers toward a rallying recovery, is a test of character and personal courage.

When we are denied, battered and afflicted, our life is often tried on this altar of endurance, the touchstone of character. It is easy to be happy and peppy and to enjoy life on a Thanksgiving Day, when the golden turkey is whole and inviting. Anyone can be in a good mood when the choice is really no choice but choice cuts. The real test of a housewife is to take the broken bones and battered flesh of leftover turkey and remake it into a tasty palatable and appetizing dish.

THE LEFTOVER TURKEY RECIPE FOR LIFE

All of us, at one time or another, come face to face with the challenge of what we consider life's leftovers. But the real test of life is not in how we behave on a Thanksgiving Day of fullness and pleasure, but on how we handle ourselves on the day after. When we are given home pleasures, birthday gifts, financial successes, glory and delight, it takes little effort to be happy. But when we have to handle a "broken bone," loss, sorrow, loneliness, defeat—when we are stripped bare like a holiday bird after Thanksgiving— it requires courage, wisdom and character to be festive and serene.

Perhaps it is difficult for young people, in the prime of life and in the zenith of personal health and success, to appreciate the full meaning of this wisdom. But even they may come to appreciate the reality of life's unfairness— that we are not always served choice cuts and we have to make do with whatever is at hand and "rehash" it into the tasteful "hash" that is our opportunity to recreate. For every life requires a leftover turkey recipe: the ability to pick up whatever is left us in life and start anew. We may even surprise ourselves as we discover that we have turned weakness into new strength, disadvantage into personal resiliency, failure into spurring fortitude, grief into extended sympathy.

Every person is bound to face loss: loss of opportunity, loss of business, loss of health, loss of companionship, loss of a dear one. But all is not lost if you still have something left in yourself—that everything in life: character. For whatever you may have lost in life, if you are still capable of giving—giving something, even as intangible as a smile—you still have what it takes to make life worthwhile living. In the end, character is really the authentic you that no one can take away from you but yourself. You see, character is an amazing quality: It succeeds without success; it prospers without prosperity; it triumphs most in failure. All it needs is you. And all you need is—it.

Too often people fail to act their part in life because they succumb to "stage fright" living. Their character is faltering as the curtain rises. They run with their lives—

from themselves, from their mission in life. They shrink in the face of responsibility and retreat into their own shell of stale withdrawal.

Perhaps no one alive is perfectly adjusted to be immune from fear and self-doubt and reticence. Such would indeed be a deadly condition. The totally adjusted person is in the grave; and lack of personal agitation and restlessness is in the tombstone. But the excessive fear that makes a person run and prevents him from plunging into the mainstream of life, is nothing short of self-affliction and self-banishment. Life involves chance; chance involves freedom and courage. A person who is afraid to take chances in life, who is timid and threatened by the margin of error, remains a psychic invalid. In his weakness and sense of insecurity, he always finds it necessary to prove himself in order to justify his faltering timidity and pretentious boldness; criticism to him is anathema; error is menacing catastrophe.

WHAT MADE JONAH RUN?

Because the victors in life are not those who succeed in pleasing everybody and in doing everything perfectly, but in having the courage to displease some and to make mistakes as they stand for something. In order to succeed, one has to learn the art of failing and surviving defeat. A person who runs away from himself is prompted by fear. He is afraid to be found mistaken lest it be called failure; forgiving lest it be taken as weakness. He is afraid to be afraid—he won't admit it—to lose face. He will therefore adhere to mulish stubbornness and seldom improve, forgive himself, or others. Such a man was Jonah the prophet. The

Book of Jonah describes the tragedy of the fugitive man
of God who sought to run away from the presence of God
and from himself.

The minor prophet had a message, a mission in life: to
extend himself in human involvement. He was told by
God to preach to the inhabitants of Nineveh, "the great
city," to repent and return from their evil ways so that they
might be forgiven and spared destruction. But Jonah was
reluctant to deliver this prophetic message out of fear that
his warning might indeed be heeded and the Ninevites
would relent and thus prove him to be the fool rather than
the prophet. Jonah, thereupon decided "to flee unto Tarshish
from the presence of the Lord."

What really happened to Jonah that made him run?
Could it be that the prophet was so uncompromising in his
stern demand for the strict disciplines of order and justice
that he failed to invoke love and mercy? Was he so heartless a prophet that he had no lovingkindness in his heart?
The nature of the man and his avocation hardly suggests
this. His character, on the contrary, is depicted as the gentle
soul who would want no one else to suffer for his mis-
adventures, suggesting: "Take me up, and cast me forth into
the sea. . . ."

Perhaps the tragedy of Jonah was not his lack of empathy
and concern for people but rather his failure to communicate
it. His inadequacy in love was not his shortage of it, but
his inability to extend it. He was afraid. A fearful person
is not free in his feelings. The poor prophet wanted to be
righteous, but he knew not how; he wanted to be loving,
but he wasn't free. He panicked. He ran. And in running
ended up in ultimate isolation, in the belly of the great fish.
This too, is to be understood in the spiritual and psychological
terms of the frantic personality of the prophet. The belly

of the great fish into which Jonah was swallowed up is to be interpreted symbolically, as a means of retreat in the face of crushing burden and responsibility. Refusing to face the obligations that life has apportioned him, he sought refuge in childish escape—the warmth and innocence of womb's existence, a condition of insensitivity to the ethical possibilities and responsibilities of a mature man.

So desperate and fearful and anguished was Jonah the man, the fugitive prophet, that his suicidal tendencies found expression in crying agony: "O Lord, take, I beseech Thee, my life from me. . . ." Jonah's ultimate running culminated in the cowardly act of seeking to end his life. Because he was not free to extend himself in personality and to love freely, he felt useless. He felt sorry for himself and blamed others for his tough luck. He sought relief in doing away with himself.

A prophet, a failure—what a tragedy. Another prophet (Micha) found it much easier to live, to reconcile, to fulfill. It was in that one therapeutic word of personal spiritual and psychological flexibility: "Return."

FOLLOW YOUR OWN STAR

The object lesson of life and experience is: Don't run! Get a hold of yourself before it's too late. Become the Columbus of your own soul to find in yourself, in the words of Sir J. Stevens, "a continent of undiscovered character."

True, it takes more courage than we can imagine to become the architect of our character and soul. For the multitudes of mass-man in a mass-society are scarcely more than strangers to themselves. They find it more convenient to run after the outermost fashion of exterior conformity rather than the innermost passion of inward individuality.

Like fleeing Jonahs they run, and running becomes a habit, a way of life, a destiny, until they are afraid to be themselves and uncomfortable in being unlike others. They look at themselves instead of into themselves and seek to please other tastes because they have lost taste in themselves and have a second-hand life, with little individual uniqueness and originality.

There are many second-hand men walking the streets because they fail to define themselves, to affirm themselves, to tune-in on themselves. They run like the proverbial man in the ad, who is a bundle of energy without direction, because a spring is hooked on to his back and he's all wound-up in exploding velocity. We recognize such men in Oscar Wilde's description when he says that "Most people are other people. Their thoughts are someone else's opinions, their lives a mimicry, their passions, a quotation."

The timorous soul, shrinking from fear of getting to know and confront himself, is devoid of courage to relate and mingle with others and is captive of a house of bondage in which strangers reside—outer images, strange gods, imitation characters. Jonah-like tossed in a sea of fear and engulfed by a whale of imaginary threats, the making of his own tempestuous mind, he sinks ever deeper into the black deep of murky crosscurrents that envelop him.

The tension of being human, it must be admitted and recognized, is real. There is a legitimate and healthy struggle within us in our duality of being. Like stars, each of us must shine in our own light and not, like a moon, reflect the light of another star. And yet, all individual stars, if they are not to burn and wink out of existence, must be arrayed in a system of constellations and galaxies within a rhythmic pattern and order that will reflect their cosmic unity and balanced orbit.

The cosmic creature, man, can take his lesson from the stars themselves, in which the shining worlds are the actors, the universe is their stage and their adventure is nothing short of eternity. The drama of human life is much like the drama of the universe itself—a death in life and a life in death. Stars are born and stars die. And as the ashes of one star give rise to a newer star, so does human life depend upon the galaxies of eternal life. (The characteristics of my life and your life have already lived in the ancestral life of Methuselah.) Each person, a world by himself, depends upon the other worlds of people, as he hangs on to his precarious existence and life-brightness.

And while we must shine brightly in our own individual stars, with all the light and warmth of our fire, we cannot dislodge our star from our human constellation and escape our system, or we shall end up in ashes like a falling star. We must equate, in time and in space, the workings and movements of our own life-support system and hitch our little space-chariot to the other stars in the universe, as we rise with our comrades, as heavenly bodies in a bright firmament.

And the fuse to this exciting human adventure lies in ourselves. For only by the cultivation of our character and our personal experience will we be able to telescope our sights toward such vision, in this the greatest drama of man: to partake of the universe and see our role in it as we extend ourselves with our fellowmen in a march toward the stars. For in character it is not so important what a man is doing for himself as what he is trying to do with himself: not so much to know where he may go but for what he must stand; not when he may arrive but what he may take along with him; not with what he lives, but what lives in him. For while success is in taking, character is in giving. And in this adventure the stars are not the limit.

7.

GIVING BIRTH TO
ONE'S SELFHOOD

*Resolve to be thyself: and
know that he
Who finds himself, loses
his misery.*
　　　　—Matthew Arnold

AS ALL PEOPLE WOULD, THE SHOELESS SA'DI OF THE
Middle Ages justly felt bitter over the lack of the simple
amenities of life. "I wept because I had no shoes," he
apologetically observed one day, "then I met a man who
had no feet." The poor old man, in deeper comprehension,
later sensed profound gratitude over himself. Instead of
complaining of being shoeless, he was grateful for not being
legless.

This human comprehension of self-sufficiency and self-
appreciation is a quality frightfully lacking in modern life.
We are in constant motion and emotion, with synthetic
smile and style, but beneath it all there is a hollow cry
and shallow action. We play our role as is expected of
civilized folk, but when the curtains rise and the act begins,
there is something missing. True, everything is ready and
moving according to scenario and plan, only that the main
character often fails to appear on the stage—our self-
character remains hidden in the costumes of clowns and
masked in the conformity of riches or rags—leaving us with

an indistinguishable mark of identity. And putting on an act doesn't stop with the outside world alone. We get into the habit and mimic our own public mimicry in the privacy of our secret lives, and as we "disguise ourselves to others . . . we disguise ourselves to ourselves" in the end.

We worry too much about things. We care too much about what others think of us. We are afraid to be left out, so we engage in stupefying socials that bore us and in deadly little games that never deceive us. But we keep on running anyhow.

We have a passion for fashion, for making it, for the status symbol, for all the frill and external embellishments that are intended to please mostly others; for shallow success, even if it kills us. What a poverty of mind there is in the richness of things where the central figure of the "I" is almost completely left out.

Perhaps man's most damning indictment before the Throne of Judgment will come to him not in the shape of fat devils jumping over him with accusing finger, but in the slow emergence of a hell in the form of that gossamer-like, puny, undernourished self that was never given a full chance in life. For the greatest tragedy in life stems not so much from what we fail to do for others, but from what we fail in ourselves: missed opportunities, wasted life, self-rejection.

Lewis Mumford points to the core of our dilemma when he ruminates on modern man's distractions: "He functions as a distracted atom in a growing chaos made poor by his wealth, made empty by his fullness, reduced to monotony by his very opportunities for variety." How poor a rich man can be, how impoverished an affluent society can prove, when the individual self is shriveled to unappreciated worth because he is buried in a pyramid of things and lost in lust, which in turn generate more ambition for more things and greater desire and greed. It's a witch-circle feeding on its own consuming power, in a merry-go-round chase.

Our task therefore must begin with the cultivation and appreciation of one's self: with the knowledge that God made all of us different so that we remain unique and original in our own character and disposition. Imitation is not our goal. And if some feel unworthy in their own importance and development, it is only because they have never reached down below their own surface to draw upon their inner strength, their deeper resources, their self- abiding fortitude. They have chosen to imitate the lives of others which show only the gloss of appearance, not the profile of character that remains concealed in their own secret selves.

Our self-acceptance, self-worth and self-appreciation will come to us by recognizing what we are in ourselves, in the value of our own living: in the simple gifts of life and limb, mind and feeling, vision and sensation, encounter and expression. Our true life is in our inward being, not in our external processions and possessions. We are original copies of the Creator. No two persons are born quite alike. There are no human carbon copies. God meant it to be this way; why then defraud Him of His work, and yourself of yourself!

Our plan on this planet, we know, is not to be someone else, someone we are not capable of being. Each person is asked to be only his best self, nothing more and nothing less. For by being his best self, he will discover his self best.

"... LET US MAKE MAN ..."

"Let us make man," thundered God's voice across the empty void, whatever that may have been. To whom did He speak and for whose assistance did He call in making that historical mammal, man, in His own image?

He spoke, I believe, to potential man, as He held that lump of matter to fashion it after His likeness: I will endow you with the gifts of self, with a waking intelligence, with an experiencing consciousness, with an indwelling spirit and soul. But your task, man, is to fulfill that potential self within you into a creative selfhood, constantly unfolding and developing to full realization.

Human life was never meant to be the creation of a full-blown perfect model, sprung from the head of God, immaculate and flawless. Man is in the making until the last rhythm of his fluttering heart is stilled. And the totality of a lifetime underlies his struggle for selfhood.

For while the endowment of self is a gift, a God-miracle, the primacy of selfhood is an achievement, man's wonder and realization. The miracle is man: a small heap of bones and tissues, organs and nerves, glands and some gray matter called brain: a marvelous system of interconnected and interchangeable activities, sensations and feelings. But what sparks the charges, the impulses that flow into our nerves to ignite in us the awareness of our consciousness, the recollections of our memories, the senses of our emotions? Ask the biochemist, the physiologist and inquire by what process is intelligence dripping in our skull, in the manner that bile is secreted by the liver, enabling us to capture sights, think thoughts and stroll back into the generations of the cloudy past and into the misty future of generations yet unborn? You seek answers, refine definitions and come, at last, to define the indefinable and explain the inexplainable in a word: miracle!

That enthralling self is God's creation and credit should be given to Him alone. But the unfolding of a creative and conscious selfhood is man's work; this is his achievement, his glory, his wonder.

As we exercise our humanity and bring into full play the conscious awareness of our total personality, we stand God-like on Olympian heights. The Alps, the oceans, the planets, in all their impressive splendor, seem so conspicuously mute in themselves. A deadly melancholy of "senseless nonentities," of cold and startling immensities! They are what they are in their static selves alone. They know not of themselves, neither do they care about others. Not so man. Puny as he appears, he is the only creation with a limitless potential for the "I."

"I" can embrace the whole world and experience the space relationships and time zones. "I" am in the universe, but the universe is also in the consciousness of "I." "The light," Fichte said, "is not without me, but within me, and I myself the light."

The "I" must be unveiled in a selfhood of original form, unrepeatable and uncomparable. "I" am the exclusive property of my individual person. I am affirming, denying, accepting, rejecting. I have a diary of my own, a private world and experience that can't be delegated to someone else. No one can step into my personal identity, nor take away my human birthright, in completing myself, in fulfilling myself, in accomplishing that work which God had begun in me, with me: "Let us make man . . ." I can experience myself, I can create myself.

I, as far as I know, I alone, among other creatures, am witness to the Creator's imperial majesty and splendid immensity. I am still central, if not center, in creation, for I am testimony to the recognition of my intelligence. God needs me even as I need God. I am man because of myself, but I am more than what I am because I have a selfhood, awaiting my development in being the Creator's creator at work, affirming myself in the "sober certainty of waking bliss."

THE VICE OF SELF IGNORANCE

The Roman philosopher, Boethius, was not exaggerating when hundreds of years ago he warned his contemporaries: "In other living creatures ignorance of self is nature; in man it is vice." Worse yet, it is self-destructive.

Self-ignorance inevitably leads to self-affliction and self-denial. Because a person who has no real awareness of himself and of his needs will soon deny himself his legitimate and necessary requirements to keep body and soul alive in unitive harmony, and thereby constrict his total personality. His unfulfilled potentialities, the need for personal fulfillment and the reality of his self-repression, will cause him neurotic conflict and misery. His unused powers will bring upon him the inner torment which will make him turn against himself by sinking in morbid self-rejection, futility and self-strangulation. He will be anguished by the distemper of intellectual shrinkage echoed in William Blake's classic warning: "He who desires but acts not, breeds pestilence." Because "Energy is Eternal Delight."

The malady of neurotic conflict in our society is conspicuous by the absence of creative and inspirational activities in the life of the individual. There is a void in the individual's inner sanctum; there is a lack of unity and dignity of personal worth, of inward integration; there is a separateness in the soul, a bleak and shadowy emptiness in the dark cave of his hidden self from whence crawl forth slimy, creeping things of thwarted ambitions, constricting fears, stifling inhibitions; irrational impulses of restlessness; irritability, and a general distaste for life.

Neurotic fear, modern psychologists explain, is real. But the person who is afflicted with it is masking himself and his true feelings—from himself, against himself. He is its first victim: so completely trapped and subverted from his true personality and self that he is unconscious of the dehumanization that takes place within him. He conspires in committing self-suicide on the installment plan. He lives without the enjoyment of life; he works without the satisfaction of creative fulfillment; he is affectionate without being affected and responsive; he seems sociable without extending himself in relatedness. He may even be successful without the pleasure of success. For he is so bound up in the struggle of inner conflicts that his energies are dissipated and wasted. He is fighting that battle of self-survival which "amounts to a supreme terror of being split apart."

The insights of religion and psychology can bring us to new discoveries, revelations and experiences of selfhood. We can shed our exterior subjective selves to witness the light of objective truth, to discover some new ethical and divine possibilities of standing "outside ourselves"—in the ecstasy of realizing our total personalities by losing ourselves in some great cause or endeavor, so that in the end we may find our true selves.

All of us can witness the wonder of the Burning Bush in the arid desert of what may be a meaningless and unfulfilled existence. Each human person has the potential for the revelation of inward bliss, of gazing at the Burning Bush of the indwelling spirit, of encountering that illuminating presence which will inspire us with an afterglow to sustain us for many days to come.

Such sights may be rare. Such revelations may seldom come. But when we do glimpse them, we know that we have been transfixed to experience the awareness of our total personality and power. We have unsandaled the shoes of our outer carping self and are hushed to respond to wonder, with awe and exaltation. For we have seen the glory of God that resides in us. And we have savored the miracle of the Burning Bush which has illumined our horizon; because for a few brief and fleeting moments we have stood alone, within ourselves, to be bathed in the light of its everlasting glory and power.

MEET THE REAL PERSON IN YOURSELF

There are those who claim that we live in a twilight zone of civilizations. We have left the dream-like garden of pastoral calm and lowly beasts but we have not yet come fully to enjoy the tempting fruits of the tree of knowledge and science. We look upon our lost innocence as a primitive condition of nature. Yet, with all our modernity and sophistication, we are still awed by the "flaming sword" and know no peace.

Man floats in weightless speed in an orbit between heaven and earth. He knows he will never return to his native simplicity and ignorance; he knows he cannot allow his conscienceless machines to outsoar him, to determine the pace and the mode of his life. Yet, the race is close and the pace is ruthless.

Persons today are too mechanized and too specialized to maintain the integrity and freedom of their personality and life. They are estranged from themselves and hopelessly alienated from the unity that underlies their inner peace.

Elements in our society conspire against the individual, explains Dr. F. A. Weiss, and tend to foster emotional conflict and mental anguish. "More and more of us—book-keepers, clerks, accountants, factory hands—are confined to a routine of fixed hours and often monotonous tasks, and become entangled in a great web of dependency. But at the same time we are forced to compete and be aggressive in a steadily increasing degree." This condition ultimately results in a social "compression chamber" of untold agony to the individual. "He resents the dependency, and feels hostility coming up; but his hostility is repressed, not only for reasons of external security, but because it contradicts his ideal self-image of himself as a good, socially-minded citizen. So he swallows his resentment and this swallowing is more important in the causation of gastric ulcers than the swallowing of rough or hard food."

And this self-mutilation similarly occurs when people feel compelled to live their lives in such a manner as to please others more than to please themselves and to live by the fashion of time more than by the fusion of faith: to fit the "pattern" and to become socially acceptable; to be popular at the cost of principle and to gain the coveted status symbol at the price of serenity, the pinnacle of a misguided sense of belonging. For what are some of those glamorized socials and glittering parties if not empty rituals of modern image-worshippers who have lost their souls and are in a mad chase after their own tails in an attempt to recapture their lost identity!

Many of them are tribal games that people play because other people play them who have seen still others play them. They are soul-eclipsing gatherings of shallow nonsense and small non-talk, mentally stifling and emotionally stupefying. And yet the social instinct to conform, the temptation to be part of the crowd prompts countless individuals to indulge excessively in such merry-go-wilds and to "swallow" many rough and indigestible mental "hors d'oeuvres" with social grace.

Few people have the courage and conviction to react the way the great French writer Balzac did when he felt repulsed after returning home from a long and uneventful party with boring people. He erected himself in front of his lined book shelves, exclaiming with excitement and relief: "Now for some real people!"

And the first among the real people one must meet is the real person in himself. Surely people have a need to be with other people. But, first and foremost they must be with themselves. The desire to be like others, to be popular, to be loved, is normal and worthwhile. But if we can't be good to ourselves, what good are we to others? And if we can't appreciate our own self worth and esteem can we hope to recognize the individual value of others? In the sage words of the ancient Talmudist Hillel: "If I am not for myself, who is for me? And if I am only for myself, what am I?"

Imitation, we know, is not our brand, nor conformity. Originality is our destiny, and thus is our identity. And in this mass society and mass identification of ours, the ancient truth of "Know thyself!" might better be modified to answer the needs of our time in finding ourselves and our individual identity first by heeding the newer motto: "Meet thyself!"

THE NEED FOR REDISCOVERY IN LIFE-BIRTH

What is a person's greatest need in life? After satisfying his physiological being and biological needs, his greatest compulsion is growth: to become. But whereas a beast of burden, a flower, a tree, develop simply by existing, a person has to nourish the deepest roots of his being in order to become. Unlike other forms of life, his development is not automatic and granted. To fulfill his destiny, he must transcend himself by extending his relationships beyond the narrow world and life of himself.

Fulfilling growth—in soul more than in body—is a necessary condition of human life and human happiness. And it is not measured in pounds and in inches but by the intangibles of the spirit.

In a true sense, this constantly new-found rediscovery of a person's hidden powers and his freshly gained perspectives, are a process of continual rebirth and self-resurrection. The human elements and the potentials are always there; only by turning our visionary powers inwardly and by rearranging the kaleidoscopic bits and pieces, we design the ever-changing and ever-glinting mosaics of renewed beauty and ecstasy. It's as if we would turn the mind's light upon itself the way a cell would look at itself.

And this can prove to be the profoundest joy of all human experiences: the superlative qualities of human encounter that allow us not only to "be lived" like the lower forms of life but to live as gods; not only to love in the flesh but also to be loved in soul; not only to be creatures of God but also to be creators with God, in fashioning things of beauty and in glimpsing moments of truth. We can extend ourselves into the lives and loves of others. We can reason, not only know. We can feel with others, not only for ourselves. We have a soul, a conscience, an intelligence and an impulse—if not always the inclination—for good. We are personalities seeking not only God but also endeavoring to imitate His eternal qualities by being God-like. However, this kind of human being demands the uninterrupted growth of becoming.

Erich Fromm refers to this experience of the daily probing self-awareness and rediscovery as a long and continuous life-birth of a lifetime: "The whole life of the individual," he writes, "is nothing but the process of giving birth to himself; indeed, we should be fully born, when we die— although it is the tragic fate of most individuals to die before they are born."

What a poor prospect, what a humiliating experience, one might contend, to struggle through life only to give full birth to one's self! Is this really the best that life can offer us mortals: to stagger for a lifetime, enduring toil and tribulation only to experience the agonizing travail of giving birth to oneself and ultimately die when we are fully developed and finally "born" in our zenith of wisdom and maturity? What an outrageous waste! What a hopeless condition! What an ungodly act!

Yet upon closer examination, we find that the inner joy of self-renewal and the experience of discovering newly born vitality and freshness is the only redeeming salvation that lies within us, and ahead of us. Of all the animal kingdom, man is the only bored creature—the most restless and searching, the most curious and uninhibited. He would literally die from the boredom of keeping his own company, or turn insane by the maddening routine of daily chores, were it not for his powers of self-innovation. His ability to gain a sense of newness, a feeling of "being born again" in the revealing reality of change and revitalization, is his only mitigating redemption. Man with an experiencing soul must have the power to re-create himself, daily. And when he does, he fulfills the destiny of that selfhood within him that cries out for redeeming growth—for the miracle of a personal exodus, free and unshackled.

THE CONSPIRACY OF A BORROWED PERSONALITY

The bitter cry of the generations for self-acceptance is the wailing trauma of our age also.

The need to get along with one's self is not satisfied by the comfort, convenience and luxury of modern sophistication. And easy access to a good time is not necesarily the gate of promise to the good life. Moreover, the many choices and possibilities of our free society and the rapid changes in our culture make of our conscience a crippled culprit, rather than an unwilling coward. We are willing to listen to the voice of conscience, but we often don't recognize which of the shouting sounds speaking to us is speaking also for us, echoing the sentiments of our soul. Adjustment, the dressmaker of all time, can hardly keep up with the new fashions and fads of our time to make the alterations that are necessary for our personal well-being and self-acceptance.

Is self-acceptance still possible for us moderns? It is, if we learn to meet ourselves on our own personal terms, knowing our limits and surrendering to our limitations. We must leave the world of goods and gods that are worshipped by the faceless and nameless masses as we cling to the personal choice of our conscience as our supreme guide and light. The non-self conformity, whether it be new or old, in riches or in rags, must not corrupt our individual taste and choice. Neither must we compete against anyone but ourselves in setting up attainable goals and practical standards of self-fulfillment. For if we demand too much of ourselves, we will be cruel and inconsiderate of the limits of our individual nature and capabilities. And if we expect too little of ourselves, we will fall short of our potential gift for development and growth and remain unfulfilled. In either case, the torment of the soul will prove unbearable and unpardonable.

The wisdom of ages, as the necessity of our time, whispers to us in edifying refrain: Be yourself, trust yourself by allowing your personality to unfold totally into the man you want to be. Be gentle with yourself. Don't tear yourself apart by doing what is not in your nature to be doing. Be loving to yourself. Don't permit grudges, petty frustrations and past wrongs to consume your vital powers with guilt, to envenom the healthy circulation of your relationships with others.

Forgive yourself, for you are only human; and if you can't put up with yourself, how can you expect others to befriend and tolerate you. Be good to yourself; for if you have the right attitude toward yourself, you will know it and the whole world will not fail to recognize it, as you will reflect a right attitude toward others as well. It will be imprinted in the large writ of your countenance and disposition and dipped in the clear conscience of your soul.

Revere yourself not by the vanity of self-worship but by the solemnity of self-esteem. You are a personality in your own right, in your unique God-given grace. You must not have an image personality borrowed from others. The compounded interest of such a conspiracy, in terms of your own worth and person, can lead to nothing short of personal bankruptcy and individual crisis.

Be you—all of you to yourself and to others—not a mere load of sleeping potentialities, but a bundle of awakening and joyous fulfillment in personality and in living.

Say with Noel Coward and believe what you're saying: "My importance to the world is relatively small. On the other hand, my importance to myself is tremendous. I am all I have to work with, to play with, to suffer and to enjoy. It is not the eyes of others that I am wary of, but my own. I do not intend to let myself down more than I can possibly help, and I find that the fewer illusions I have about myself or the world around me, the better company I am for myself."

You may not set the world on fire, but you can save it from becoming a cosmic torture chamber by saving your soul and by becoming what you are destined to be—yourself. If you like in yourself what you have, you may someday have in yourself what you like in others.

"INDIVIDUAL REDEMPTION . . .
EARNED EVERY DAY"

Unfortunately, many people want to be like most other people, when they should want to be most like themselves, in discovering the best within them.

Discover yourself anew, every day of your life, if you wish to grow up before growing old and stale before your time. A person can be an unbearable bore, especially to himself whose presence he cannot escape, unless he can discover new depths of vitality and the saving powers of self-regeneration.

People who run away from themselves, who seek to escape the level of reality, are empty and unhappy inwardly because they lack the healthy appetites and stimulations of creative and excitable life-experiences. They seek meaning and fulfillment outside themselves because they cannot find it within themselves.

They have failed to delve inwardly to tap their most welling waters of individual salvation and self-extension. Their vital sources of life have dried up.

"Individual redemption, like a livelihood," says Eleazar, "must be earned everyday." And it is not an automatic endowment from the heavenly powers above. It comes by merit and is bestowed upon all who wish to direct their thoughts and labors by eliciting the redemptive grace of the Creator—who is neither biased nor favoring the few—here and now, on this earth, in the context of everyday life.

The messianic powers are within reach of all. They are nearest and in ample abundance in ourselves—not in the remoteness of promise, but in the immediacy of fulfillment —offering us spiritual and physical regeneration in a troubled age. It is at a time such as ours, in an age of social unrest and cataclysmic change that the individual person finds himself lost and forgotten. (This was true also during the rise of Christianity and at the inception of Hasidism, when the search for individual redemption gave birth to new mystical religious orientations.)

There is today a quest for the messianic grace that will promise individual redemption from an oppressive social climate that ignores the masses and offers little hope for individual freedom and self expression. This is evidenced in the cry of the older generation and in the rebellion of the younger generation.

Clearly, it is to the host of forgotten men and women and young adults that the prophetic message of faith speaks: Salvation comes in personal savings accounts. It is a feel-it-yourself business. It is a most democratic system, a system in which the process of blissful redemption is a "serve your-self" undertaking and in which no special qualifications are necessary. The only requirement to hitch our chariot to a star, is the will to partake of this all-pervading adventure of life by making it work to the maximum of our ability. And we can make it work by the internalizing and by the psychologizing of the ancient wines of salvation within our newer vessels of modernity.

". . . I WILL BE WHAT I WILL BE"

We recall in biblical narrative how Moses sought a clear communion sign, a definitive approach to communication with the God-forces of redemption. He felt that the re-deeming capability by which man must abide should be readily definable, easily invoked and identified by all.

But Moses was rebutted by a terse explanation instead

of a clear definition: ". . . I will be what I will be." (The traditional translation, "I am what I am," from the original, lacks precision. *"Ehye asher ehye"* in Hebrew literally means "I will be what I will be.")

In this short and self-identifying description of the Divine lies, perhaps, the whole prospect of man's redemption. Moses was told for all time: man, redemption does not come from the outwardness of foreign powers, but from the inwardness of inner strength, self-radiating and self-regenerating.

". . . I will be what I will be," God says to man. I will be what every person finds me to be to himself; what every individual soul makes me to be within himself; what every man makes of himself to be, by allowing the divine spirit to become a steady resident of his soul, in shaping his thoughts, his daily life and his ultimate destiny.

God, individual salvation, redemptive grace, are not dictionary definitions, or worded formulas, but rather they are the dialect of the soul. And as you are unable to describe the soul, you can't define its thought processes of communication. One thing is clear: The gate to individual salvation is open to all the common and forgotten people of whom Lincoln spoke as being loved by God because he created so many of them. Moreover, this grace cannot be bought or achieved by power, position or wealth.

All we need is to believe in ourselves and in that part of the Messiah which is implanted within us, making it possible for us to elicit those redeeming powers that will restore to us the harmonies of heaven and earth and bring healing to both body and soul. And when we come to experience such mystical ecstasy, we gain a joyous and cheerful affirmation of the goodness of life and the worthwhileness of our individual purpose in living.

We can't see God, but we can have a vision of Divinity. By making ourselves visible to Him, we find Him in our hearts. And those who believe that God speaks only to them and that His salvation is the favored monopoly of a select few, have adopted for themselves a very small and marginal God with a dwarfed soul for His residence.

God is not some men; God is all men. God is not in my faith alone; God is in all faiths: in all who sincerely believe in His kingdom and His glory and His majesty and in the power He placed in our hands to make this kingdom a beautiful garden in which the variegated flowers of many colors, shades and shapes shall flourish in all their splendid array and uniqueness. And behold! Among them, all-feeling and reasoning and knowing, is that marvelous "I."

Descartes summed it up this way: "I think, therefore I am." Not "I am what I am," but I am what I make of myself: I am what I think, I am what I feel, I am what I believe, I am what I envision, I am what I dare, I am what I dream, I am to God what I am to myself. I am to myself what I am to others. My selfhood makes me a whole man. And my manhood makes humanity whole and holy.

W. Macneile Dixon speaks of material things as senseless nonentities because they can never become conscious of themselves and are therefore incapable of outsoaring themselves and rise above their sources. But man is different. "The 'I,'" he said, "is the window through which every man that ever was born looks out upon the scene of existence. Flung open at his birth, shuttered at his death, at this window through which no one else can ever look, this untransferable viewpoint, each one of us sits all his life long."

8.

FAITH POWER

If the stars should appear one night in a thousand years, how men would believe and adore, and preserve for many generations the remembrance of the City of God which had been shown!
—Ralph Waldo Emerson

IN THE DARK DEPTH OF A PRISON WALL, AN INSCRIPTION was found which can enlighten many of us. It was a most fervent affirmation of faith: "I believe in the sun, even when it is not shining; I believe in love, even when feeling it not; I believe in God, even when He is silent."

Isn't this what faith is really all about: believing where understanding has failed, envisioning where sight is dimmed, groping where there is dark silence, loving even while love is veiled in memory instead of being nestled in the heart?

What is faith? Faith is an adventure, a dialogue, an involvement, a dynamic encounter with the highest, a coming-alive full of strength, a responsiveness of living to the fullest.

In faith, we are neither passive in receiving nor bitter in resisting. We accept while we ask questions, even at the risk of disillusionment. We may be alone when in faith, but never lonely. We may be wrestling with our conscience by probing and doubting, but we can always rest reassured in our sincerity of belief by endorsing Tennyson's conviction that "there lives more faith in honest doubt . . . than in half the creeds."

Are we clinging today to half creeds, believing what we

want to believe, seeing what we want to see, hearing what we want to hear? It seems as if everything is so fleetingly transitory in our life, everything is so rapidly changing that abiding faith is laid to rest, "bedridden in some dormitory of our souls."

We look around us and see how faith can be blind if it is more self deluding than self-doubting; how trust can be misplaced if it's coined in silver and copper alone. For profit is not growth, success is not salvation, security is not serenity, formula is not faith. And if doing is believing, then our voracious hustling is our true yardstick, reflecting upon the condition of our faith, which is indeed dormant and "bedridden in some dormitory of our souls."

We seem to have loosened our grip of faith and our uncompromising attachment to what generations before us considered absolute values. Like Shakespeare's character, many a modern "wears his faith but as the fashion of his hat; it ever changes with the next block." He changes his set of views and scale of values as fast as he changes outworn rags, embracing a conformity of thought so convenient and total as to remain unnerved and dehumanized in mass society. He clings to the transitory instead of the abiding, to the commercial instead of the spiritual, to fiction instead of enduring faith.

Change, indeed, happens to all of us. We cannot control it but neither must we allow it to control us. We must be riding along with the vicissitudes of time, but move at our own pace, lest we outpace the man in us and become blindly harnessed to time's run-away chariot. We want to live with the times, but without letting life pass us by and leave us self-mutilated and deprived of our individual worth.

Many among us are sterile in their creative life, stifled in conviction—cowardly afraid. They pretend to fear no one and nothing; and act it, aggressively. Yet, inwardly they are neurotic. They clown in the skin of lion's courage, loud and strong; but it's only a bark. Fear paralyzes them because they have lost the chemistry of their faith. (Newer tubes have become more fashionable.) They have no faith in God, who can speak to them in silence; they have no faith in man, who can relate to them in love; they have no faith in themselves, who alone can unleash the inner reactor of their atomic power.

Faith, to use a current phrase, is a do-it-yourself business. It must begin with the individual self. And it must concern itself with the real things of life, things that reside within us, not outside; in value of the spirit, not in valuables of accumulation; in things that are not visible, yet as real and as powerful and as priceless as anything on earth. Because the greatest monuments we can build are those of character and spirit; and the holiest shrines we can erect are those of the heart and soul—shrines upon whose altars the eternal flame of faith's holy light will forever be kept burning.

FAITH'S LASER-LIKE POWER

Improvement, someone keenly observed, begins with "I." Identity, I might add, also begins with "I."

This might be well worth remembering at a time when individual identity is associated with a punch card number; when belonging is reduced to a togetherness of convenience; when success is considered in terms of efficiency; and when the profit motive is stronger than the prophet's impulse. For, ironically, our very success and progress have brought us to this predicament. It is almost as if we have tasted from the tree of knowledge to be doomed only for our adventurous spirit and industry.

For while our streamlined technology and science have

unleashed for us unlimited powers and knowledge, they have not at the same time lavished upon us in equal measure the wisdom and the happiness to enjoy the fruit of our harnessed labor. And while our technological genius lifts us toward the stars, "human values are still languishing until the products of our machines themselves become empty substitutes for failing values." The individual human heart cries out for an identity—for a name in a nameless society, for a face in a faceless humanity.

The great search is on. It is not the search for gold, for power, for fame. It is a quiet quest that goes on in the hearts and minds of all men. And the quest turns into a struggle, a struggle not for wages and security and a living, but for a life of human dignity, self-worth, individual identity and purpose, for the prospect that the individual person still counts in a system that is becoming increasingly computerized and impersonal.

To the question emanating from the garden above: "Where art thou, man?" a mass of humans echo individually in a chorus of voices, some of their own perturbing questions: Who in the world am I? What is the value of my individual life in the sprawling jungle of concrete and steel? What is my purpose in a world where the good life is measured in goods and happiness in efficiency? Are we headed toward a condition in which man who has made the machine will become more and more machine-like "by a kind of diabolical inversion of the mystery of Incarnation?"

We know the answer is not in a cold skepticism of a mechanized and fossilized civilization and culture that will make us appear more like super-educated monkeys than flying angels. Our God-image lies in our individual faith and in our adventurous spirit and nature, in a search for our identity, in a groping for our destiny.

Faith is described by W. R. Inge as a solitary act, "an act

of self-consecration, in which the will, the intellect, and the affections, all have their place." It is this act of spiritual affirmation, of reason and emotion, of logic and trust that gives strength to all our endeavors and defies the impossible, thus lifting us to adoration and wonder. Faith needs no evidence. The evidence of faith is in faith itself, in all that makes us human and intelligent and worthwhile. You define faith as you define love and light: It's there, simply because you know you are there.

Faith has a power not unlike that of the concentrated laser beam that cuts through granite and sends its rays traveling to the highest distances and spheres. But its strength is in concentrated power, in consecrated light, in accumulated intensity. Faith has to be sought within the inward gleams of communion, not in the outward shouting of clamoring communication. It is within the hidden depth of one's self to be discovered.

We are taught, and our own experience and wisdom confirms it, that without faith we can do nothing; with faith there isn't anything we can't do. With faith in our hearts, life assumes meaningful purpose and design, and the living confidence to echo M. L. Hoskins' trust by saying: "I said to the man who stood at the gate of the year, 'Give me a light that I may tread safely into the unknown,' and he replied, 'Go out into the darkness and put your hand into the hand of God. That shall be to you a better light and safer than a known way.' "

"... TO DO JUSTICE,
TO LOVE MERCY AND TO WALK HUMBLY . . ."

Religious creed is not only a feeling of emotion, but also the act of faith in motion, in deed as well as in thought.

Religious faith entails a devotion of life, a commitment. And devotion is a derivative from the Latin word "to vow" implying a dynamism of commitment, a moving and rousing faith.

The ancient Hebrews, immediately upon their unfettering of the shackles of slavery, were instructed in the disciplines of sacrifice. Their newly-won freedom and redemption imposed upon them a corresponding sense of individual responsibilities and duties. Freedom demands its price, faith its exercises.

"Onward in faith!" . . . "Move forward!" is Divine's redeeming voice thundering at every crossroad of the arid desert, at every parting of the raging sea, at every exodus of man, at every crossing into the promised land of individual redemption. And children of the human race, since time immemorial, have moved onward and forward in response to that eternal voice, pioneering new frontiers and new orbits, conquering oceans of water and of space, mastering worlds within themselves—worlds of ignorance, superstition and human wilderness.

And the voice is heard time and again and is echoed in the heart of every man. It asks not for blood, for burnt-offerings, for ablutions. It asks only for those self-redeeming powers that will make man a real man, so much man as to be capable not only of the animal instinct of self-preservation but also of the God impulse of self-sacrifice, in obedience to an ideal, a cause, a principle of life.

But faith, to most of us, doesn't even require self-sacrifice. It unequivocally rejects it in everyday life as primitive paganism. Yet, too many people today are guilty of self-mutilation in one way or another, in body or in soul. They commit the sin of self-immolation by working themselves to death, by driving themselves to death, by burning out before their time in presenting themselves as burnt offerings upon some dubious altar of pleasure, plan, or ambition. "Everywhere you turn," writes Alexander Eliot, "you see people who are self-sacrifices. They are, in the main, self-sacrifices to their own insurance policies, or to their own programs; they are caught in the closets of their own perceptions."

For most average people the test of faith is not in the self-offering of dramatic and heroic achievements, but in the daily and trying experiences and chores and in the little disciplines of faith that require of us sacrifices in small measures. For, as someone wisely put it, we are not required to do great and extraordinary things; it is sufficient if we do small things extraordinarily well: if we heed the prophetic admonition and do whatever we do with heart and soul, with justice and with mercy and with humility before our God.

The simple requirements of faith are sublime, but not easy to practice. In time of crisis and danger, we usually rise to our destiny and display the best in man; yet, in ordinary daily circumstances, too often we are apt to show the beast in man: faltering indifference, selfishness and greed. As in the words of Goethe: "To make large sacrifices in big things is easy, but to make sacrifices in little things is what we are seldom capable of."

In real, dynamic and steady faith, we commit ourselves to a truth greater than our own; we submit to a power mightier than our own; we dedicate our energies to a life higher than our own mortal beings. We thus rise to a life beyond our own life, to experiences of feeling and vitality of spiritual heights ordinarily concealed from us. Faith, in practice, is more than a science; it is "love taking the form of aspiration." And as love has the power to transmute human misery and frailty into fortitude and sublimity, turning physical weakness and despondency into an inward awakening and glow, so can faith transform our life, our personality and our spirit.

WITH A SENSE OF WONDER AND REVERENCE FOR LIFE

I believe that when Albert Schweitzer enunciated his idea of reverence for life, he meant that our life must have not only a sense of reality but also the sensation of realization. Man must be not only full in stomach and satisfied, but also fulfilled in soul and sanctified.

Holiness is a dimension of life that adds realization and fulfillment to our sense of reality and fullness. By responding to the evocative Life Soul forces that animate the universe, we become part of a universal symphony of sounds and rhythms and attain the awareness to discover anew the vast harmonies of life.

Unfortunately, holiness has become a quaint and antiquated word, an outworn relic of dead shrines, a smoldering ember of dying altars. We think of holiness as clothed in the black robes of isolation and the stifling collar of the ancient monk: all gloomy, ascetic and solitary. Many of us think of holiness as the negation of a free and creative life, as a formula of self-denial and compulsory self-censorship that ultimately leads to self-stunting. One might sum it up by using a contemporary expression and say: Holiness is not fun.

True, holiness is not fun. It's a more serious and sober business. It's beauty in action, wonder in discovery, devotion in realization, faith in fulfillment, love in living and life in reverence.

But all adjectives are only words, and all attempts to

define holiness are futile unless the concept of holiness attains that prime condition without which it cannot exist: the proper mood.

The mood, the setting of the stage, the atmosphere, is what makes holiness or mocks it. Nothing great, nothing elevating, nothing inspiring, nothing worth having, is ever achieved without proper preparation and deliberate forethought. Life can shrivel into the stale routine of existence, of working to eat and eating to work—a condition that degrades the beauty of life into a struggle for a living and man's glorious prospect into an aimless drifting toward the dead end of a cosmic enigma.

What gives life life, a throbbing dimension and pulsating blood-vitality with every heartbeat of living, is our innate gift of radar power and radio communication: to scan the starry heavens and to tune in on the universe by making contact with that intelligent Life Source which sustains all living. The awareness of wonder, not for curiosity's sake alone, but for the purpose of rediscovery and renewal, lies at the very heart of holiness.

Wonder is the father of all knowledge; and with the increase of knowledge our sense of reverence and awe should deepen. The awesome knowledge of the stupendous universe outward can humble us to insignificance; but the magnificent brilliance of the reverent mood inward can elevate us to exaltation. Holiness is a keyword in our glorious reality, lifting us to adoration.

For unless we invest life with sanctity and renew it daily, we are bored to death. We are creatures of habit. But many die from habit, even before they die in habit. Change is at the root of all things, growth is in the nature of all life. A reverence for life, the creating of the holy mood, is the water of our growth, the sunshine of our beauty, the very soil to our roots.

The machine age is more a clattering and dinning age than a meditating and perceiving one. But, alas, holiness cannot be produced in synthetic plastic tubes by chemical reaction. It must radiate from the self-made fires of a Burning Bush which can illuminate deserts; from the heart-conceiving revelations of summit mountains which can enlighten civilizations; from man's ability to stop and stand in awe at the sight of wonder and listen to a voice without sound telling him: ". . . the place upon which thou standest is holy ground."

We cannot treat life with irreverence by banishing those thoughts and moods that ennoble all our experiences and give us a glimpse of that infinite life of which we are a part. There must be moments of hush and quietude in our life—moments of moody introspection, of self-reverence and self-rediscovery—when we catch glimpses of the infinite glory and the mysterious majesty that can bring reverence into our being, wonder into our experiences—all holy and wholly in our human conduct to add fullness to our life.

MIRACLES DO HAPPEN IN OUR TIME

I can never understand why some people find life so boring that they have to look for kicks and thrills in order to escape reality. As for myself, reality is miracle. The experience of the present moment is worth more than a thousand tales of magic and wonder. Thus it was to Walt Whitman, who saw miracle in every hour of light and dark in every cubic inch of space; to Voltaire, who perceived all miracle in the stupendous order of nature, the revolution of a hundred million worlds around a million suns; to W. Macneile Dixon, who sees miracles everywhere and observes nothing but the works of magic: "Nature is not natural, but supernatural, delighting in marvels. . . ."

Yet, it has all become a matter of routine for us. We have taken the familiar to become mundane, the everyday spectacle to be a bore, the wonder of the living moment in time and in space as a cosmic imbecility. We have found a convenient and useful word, "nature," to conceal deeper perceptions and meanings. We dismiss wonder, miracle and awe as the works of some stupendous "natural" compulsion and let it rest at that.

It often seems so senseless and visionless. Yet, miracle is all around us. And when we ourselves partake of the miraculous, we soar closer to our destiny. Such has been the fate of our generation when we witnessed the breathtaking glimpses of our earthlings as they closed in with their spaceships on a suspended, cratered moon in a black and awesome sky.

Who says miracles don't happen in our time? They do. And, what's more important, we have made this one happen. Think of it: We have seen in our own days not the crossing of one marshy, unpassable Red Sea, but the navigating of vast oceans of the blackest black in a stark void of the universe! We are treading where angels were believed to soar: a quarter million miles in soundless and weightless space. Who else could have done this but miracle-maker, man?

Miracle, in truth, is in the nature of man. For what is miracle if not the ability to rise above the ordinary and to do that which has been established as natural limits. But the ordinary and natural of today have been impenetrable unknowns yesterday.

The miraculous and wondrous are within the reach of every individual when he grasps the truth that with faith and resolution he faces (reasonably speaking) few limitations other than those that he alone has set for himself.

In this sense, we don't look for a miracle as an enchanting rainbow in the sky, but as an opportunity to stretch our own human powers so as to make that which seems impossible today the possibility of tomorrow. We need not invoke magical outside powers in order to see wonder, to behold revelation. We have only to release the God-powers within us to perform those God-things we call miracle.

". . . Life itself is the real and most miraculous miracle of all," said Christopher Fry. "If one had never seen a human hand and were suddenly presented for the first time with this strange and wonderful thing, what a miracle, what a magnificently shocking and inexplicable and mysterious thing it would be . . . I want to look at life—at the commonplace of existence—as if we had just turned a corner and run into it for the first time."

To see things in their new-found freshness and vitality, as if we had just turned around the corner for the first time; to take notice of wonder as if it is the first sensation in our life, that's to sense miracle. It is not nature violated and disrupted, but rather nature relished in its most natural condition through the extension of such natural powers that seemed beyond our grasp and missing hitherto. If the natural atom has such immense and unpredictable powers, can we doubt the capabilities and possibilities of miracle in our own lives! Can we fail to perceive our human strength and spirit to out-miracle past miracles!

9.

LIVING INTENSELY
IN EVERY TENSE

This is the true joy in life, the being used for a purpose recognized by yourself as a mighty one; the being thoroughly worn out before you are thrown on the scrap heap; the being a force of Nature instead of a feverish selfish little clod of ailments and grievances complaining that the world will not devote itself to making you happy.

—George Bernard Shaw

WITH THE PASSAGE OF EVERY YEAR, WE BECOME EVER-more mindful of the fleeting quality of time and ponder anew the meaning of our life on earth.

We can become saddened by the resistless onrushing waves of time and we can feel like atomic dust in an eternity of time and space. But we need not measure our significance and value in terms of last year's discarded calendar, or in the unstoppable ticking away of the clock, or in the many sunsets that lengthen our shadows. For the measure of our time on earth is best recorded in the marks we leave in memory and conscience, in the heart throb of feeling and in the glow of promise that is evoked by the sunrises that lie ahead of us. We shall not fret, remembering the wise man's adage that those who make the worst use of their time complain most of its shortness.

Time is not to be feared and regimented, but to be fully understood and experienced. It is a gift flowing from the liberal hand of the Eternal's inexhaustible stream of eternity and it is to be embraced with cheer and savored with sensitivity. We cannot mutilate it and compress it "without injuring eternity," if we are to live all the time of our life, never to feel shame or regret.

Time cannot be rushed, expanded or disjointed. Those who try to manage time with the efficiency of a ledger by crowding in dates, will soon find that the time they are struggling to manipulate is being more endured than enjoyed, more misspent than ennobled.

American efficiency and management have probably made us the most time-conscious society. We plan our time as we manage our assembly lines. We crowd our calendar with appointments and dates not only in the course of a day's work, but also in anticipating our vacation and leisure. We often overorganize, overwork and overtax ourselves unnecessarily to burdensome proportions. Overtime has become synonymous with our way of life and our mode of work. Our time schedule can be very hectic and productive, but not always very fulfilling. Put together the most beautiful notes of a song and take the "rest times" out of the score, and you'll produce an unrhythmic jingle-jumble of sounds.

Modern technology and medical science have accomplished the miracle of saving life's time and prolonging man's pilgrimage on earth. We have added more years to our life, but have we also added more life to our years? We have raised our standard of living, but have we also raised our standard of life? Have we mastered the art of using our time wisely to enable us to derive more meaning from every hour of life, or is boredom killing many of us in leisure?

The theme of modern life, much like the shock waves of contemporary beat-beat music, is too overpowering in sound and fury. The "rests" are conspicuously absent and frenetically out of joint with time; the tempo and timing is too dehumanizing, too demoralizing, too scandalizing.

We are more often occupied with the timely and practical at the expense of the timeless and eternal. We roam in the outer spaces of physical nature, but fail to enter the inner spaces of human nature. We spend too much time with the busyness of living and too little time on the business of life. Human experience requires moments of quietude when we are hushed to the secret sounds of deepening meaning and mystifying strength.

We can truly mark time by taking time out to celebrate life, to engage in the contemplative insights of human encounter by watching the sky, by observing the stars, by admiring a sunrise, by viewing a sunset, by dreaming and by feeling, by relating and reaching out from the innermost atom of self to the outermost realm of the infinite. We need time not only to be but also to become, not only for the length of days but also for the fullness of life, not only for ripeness of age but also for maturity of experience. For we can be rich in years and poor in time and experience if we waste the opportunities for life that each day offers us.

THE SOLEMN REALITY OF TODAY

We must live in the present tense, in this world and now. And, even while now hardly seems the most beautiful of times, we must nevertheless cherish the gift of the present hour, as it is ours to live in reality and experience.

Dreams are the visions of the future. Nightmares are the regrets of the past. But the life of today, in the words of Thomas Carlyle, "is no idle dream, but a solemn reality." To live in the solemn reality of today means to live life as a whole and to feel it in all its throbbing fullness of the moment as it clearly lies at hand. For living is not merely breathing impulses but breath-taking responses that fill our whole being with the dripping elements of life and the conscious awareness that opens our eyes to the visions of a greater universe and our hearts to the feelings of a nobler humanity.

In the midst of all the distractions and annoyances of life, the daily horrid grind of apprehension and of cares, we cannot fail in the central task of building our character. For the one thing we can never get away from is meeting ourselves. And since this most intimate companionship of self is the one most permanent relationship in life, it had better be a pleasant one.

The time, the only real, living and existing time, is now. For if not now, when? For now is everything. Now was yesterday, now is today and now will be tomorrow—if it be ours to dispose of. In the epigrammatic wisdom of Martial, "Tomorrow I will live, the fool does say; today itself's too late; the wise lived yesterday."

To hew a character in the present tense of today is to mold a destiny for tomorrow. And every hour is precious in the irretrievable opportunity of the moment. To the cynic who asks what can be accomplished in the short duration of a fleeting moment—we say, perhaps not much at a time, but not little in a lifetime; if it takes on a sense of destiny, of timeliness and timelessness; if life rises above the shallow and the mundane as it assumes value and adds to beauty and to the increase of happiness and to the brightening of the heart and to the scattering of light and of love and to the dispelling of darkness and of fear, of hatred and of loneliness; if life abides by the deeper voices that have stirred in Robert Herrick the cry for a fullness of life, in declaring: "Gather ye rose-buds while ye may: Old time is still flying: And this same flower that smiles today: Tomorrow will be dying."

The call for an awareness of today that sees old time flying, is probably life's most stern challenge. The waste of time of wading in past tears and guilt, in worry over things that never will be, in the gross neglect of gathering rosebuds of beauty and of grace, while we may, is life's greatest undoing. Why should death be feared and not the living-death of those who spend their time merely in breathing and brooding, in fretting and complaining, in hating the world and the living and in tolerating their own life only as a burden to themselves and as a sigh to others?

By learning to appreciate every hour for whatever it offers us and by snatching every moment with grace and gratitude, we may gather the rosebuds of a fuller and nobler life. What we give to life will come back our way. What we add to it will be credited to our living account with compounded dividends.

This will help us to avoid the predicament of that pampered lady who bitterly complained to her doctor of the night air she so utterly disliked that it became her obsession. "But madam," replied the wise physician to the disgruntled lady, "during certain hours of the twenty four, night air is the only air there is."

Surely there are hours of "night air" and moments of disquietude in our life that we may not like; yet we are expected to make the best of our time by endowing it with an acceptance of loveliness and understanding, as we look upon the larger picture of life as a whole.

The wisdom of making the most of our time lies in crowding the hour with glory, whenever possible; in appreciating the joys of the present, wherever they may be found; in a daily new-found awareness of longing to live and not merely in a desire for living long.

"... THE HOUR OF SPLENDOR IN THE GRASS ..."

Time is like a river. You never step into the same river twice. Its flowing stream always gushes forth with new tides. So is time. The forever flowing tide of time washes every moment with newness. Can we live in the past, can we wait for the future when the living present is now and new, irrevocably bursting forth into the shimmering moments of every day's awakening?

The quiet past is washed away in the river of time. The golden age of yesteryear, seen from a dim distance, is nostalgically hallowed and glorified. We find hope in the springtide of the future and longing in the receding wave of the past. But the present often holds no fascination and ardor for us. Yet, if we neglect it, we may even regret its memory in the future as a haunting past.

We should be up and doing—now. We cannot live in the past without maiming the present and stultifying the future. Life is real and vibrant if it is open to the voices of the present and not to the echoes of an outworn yesteryear.

Past glories can hypnotize us into a deadly trance; past agonies can fossilize us into stony oblivion. We think with Wordsworth that "nothing can bring back the hour of splendor in the grass, of glory in the flower." Every hour has its own unique glistening splendor that shines with a heart-warming afterglow. But as grass withers and as the flower fades, they make way for new blades and fresh flowers. It is futile to relive the past. Time, wisely lived in the opportunity of the present hour and flower—of beauty and of truth—may yet offer the new opportunities of revelation, "of splendor in the grass, of glory in the flower." As we are highly sentimental about the past, we can easily become awed by it and mesmerized.

When in biblical narration, Lot's wife fixed her gaze upon the flaming cities of Sodom and Gomorrah and looked back upon the horror and guilt of those doomed places, she turned into what became known as the proverbial pillar of salt. Dehumanized by the memory of her past life, she emerged stony, statue-like and saline, after failing to heed the voice of the present that warned: "Look not behind thee." Let bygones of the past be bygones. "Let the dead Past bury its dead!" Let the gloom and the doom and the guilt of traumatic days pass on.

But Lot's wife could not tear herself away from her former past, from her guilt associations, from her ugly humiliating shame. Subsequently, succumbing to the "dead past," her existence became as stationary and solidified as the soulless pillar of salt. She could never forgive herself, nor forget her past self.

The tragedy of Lot's wife is not hers alone. There are many, alas too many, who live in the past and look back upon a horrifying experience, a harrowing guilt, an anguishing sadness, a traumatic emotion, an ugly association. They literally become petrified and paralyzed in their responses to all life surrounding them. Instead of moving forward with the times, they look backward into the fire and brimstone of bygone upheavals. Old ghosts terrorize and brutalize them to become so mentally and emotionally mangled and twisted as to lose all capacity of leading normal and happy lives. They fail to renew life each day by wading into the river of time as it is ebbing and flowing with new tides and passing waves, past and present, moment by glittering moment, hour by precious hour, day by holy day.

It has been keenly observed that life is a jigsaw puzzle

with most of the pieces missing. If this be true, it will help little to dwell in the dark past when at hand lie the scattered "pieces" of life, all heaped in a puzzle that becomes at once the urgent business of every minute and every hour of living. Life's puzzle is perhaps staggering, but its challenges are not puzzling. It is perhaps the way John B. Tabb put it: "Every year that I live, I am more conscious that the waste of life lies in the love we have not given, the powers we have not used, the selfish prudence which will risk nothing, and which, shirking pain, misses happiness as well."

"THE FUTURE IS A WORLD LIMITED BY OURSELVES"

Those who can look upon the past with no regret and remorse can face the present with a cheerful disposition and with few complaints. They can turn to the future with confidence and without fear.

The past often seems too fast and haunting; the future appears too slow and creeping; and the present looks too petty and deceitful. In time, as in space, we see "optical illusions"; they are the creations of our own making.

Some chase the shadows of a vanishing dream, the gleams of a lonely wish that is tucked away back in the mist of time and unreality: They persist in pain. Some are dazzled by the glaring uncertainty of a new dawn breaking out on the horizon of a fresh morning that casts fear and blinds the eye: Who knows what the future will bring? But to those who are fully alive and up with the times, the wave of the future is not to be feared but glimpsed in hope and experienced in promise. They share in the exuberant optimism of Tennyson, declaring: "I dipt into the future far as human eye could see, saw the vision of the world and all the wonder that would be."

We are made noble and most human not by the lenses of our eyes but by the light of our visions, not by the things we see but by the wonders we perceive, not by the shadows of the past and the petty pace of the creeping present but by a future that is as open and as exciting as the life of an eternity.

But how futile it might be, indeed how foolish it is, to anticipate the promise of time everlasting, if we find the moment boring and the hour an intolerable burden. Why should we pray to endure in the eternity of time and life, as immortals, when we cannot tolerate the crawling moment?

The human dimension of living, the potential of fully realizing one's selfhood, lies in the total unfolding of life, in time and in space, and by hallowing both with grand nobility and with crowning glory, with a human awareness and appreciation. By leaping into the wave of the future, the present is enriched with a dreamlike quality and ennobled with yearning vision, with revealing wonder.

How wonderful is the day in which we see the tide in the spring, the beam in the light, the glow in sunshine, the silence in moontide, the burst in the flower, the "budding morrow in midnight!" How exciting it can be to leap into the wave of the future, to bathe in the stream of time, to float in the wonderland of sights and smiles and beauty and truth! How promising it can prove to look forward with trusting eyes, to discover the sweet air of evening skies, "the Sabbath of our God," the destiny and universality of man!

"The future is a world limited by ourselves" is at once a most sobering and rewarding promise, as well as a frightening and staggering responsibility. We discover it in proportion to our adventurous spirit and enduring heart, according to the breadth of our interests and the depths of our experiences. The abiding moment can have so much more meaning and perspective if we feel the high-spirited adventure of life as enunciated by Lincoln Steffens, who had the courage and the vision to say: "I have been over into the future and it works."

The future works for those who plan it, wait for it, pray for it, anticipate it, welcome it and fear it not. For they have "been over" in the life of tomorrow, with a heart of faith in the future, with an eye of vision of the shape of things to come, with a consciousness of being there—because they glimpsed the wonder of the future with the eyes of the present. They have become larger than life itself, because they have encountered a Presence today with the dream of a lovely tomorrow, a reality that is not yet in being but very much part of life in experience and revelation.

10.

ACCEPT CHANGE—LIFE'S PRECIOUS CURRENCY

May you live all the days of your life.

—Swift

IN THE CHANGE OF SEASONS, WE SEE OUR OWN HUMAN situation, with spring, summer, autumn and winter rolling in a flowing and steady stream of time.

And the wisdom of life is to accept change and to find whatever beauty and grace it possesses. The all-wise tells us: "To everything there is a season, and a time to every purpose under the sun."

Certainly it's easy to rejoice in spring, to be exuberant in summer. When all is promising and bright, warm and life-laden, smiles come lightly, laughter is abundant. But when autumn comes and moods are drooping, to sustain the joy and laughter of brighter days requires wisdom.

Autumn is usually associated with a melancholy spirit, with a sort of baleful resignation. We have enjoyed the summer in all its fullness of life. Yet it seemed so fleetingly short, so regrettably speeding for the accommodation of all our dreams. We hardly had time to savor the season, and behold it's rolling out of sight. And here we stand half-fulfilled, half-dazed, to find change coming upon us, compelling us to accept the new and alternating realities of life and of nature.

We are more than a little saddened to see flowers fading, leaves falling, light diminishing and shadows lengthening. Do we see in the life of nature, the nature of our own life?

It seems that only a short time ago, the day dawned in a longer morning, the sun glowed in fuller warmth and the night surrendered to a longer evening. Now we are compelled by seasonal change, to accept the shortcuts in daytime, sunshine and leisure. And slowly and steadily frost is felt; its first traces of white are visible.

Yet, there is a glory and splendor in autumn. If it is the end to that beginning which marked our spring, it is also the beginning to another natural pause and lapse that will eventually usher in another beginning, a new spring. Growth and decay are interchangeable. We can see a new beginning at each end. Falling leaves and decay make way for a new vitality to germinate, for a new birth of spring to come after next winter's desolation. Indeed, there is in autumn much beauty and truth to cheer the heart. If it has no heat, it has a restful serenity; if it has waning light, it has solemn depth; if it is followed by a long winter, it is surely readying for another spring and another ripening.

And if autumn could speak to us, it would tell us to surrender gracefully to change. For in surrender there is glory and strength. There is surrender in love; there is surrender in charity; there is surrender in joy and there is surrender in harmony and peace. The lesson of autumn is clear: after a summer of floral and green offering to the universe, it fears not the temporary retreat of sun, warmth and growth. The downward movement is a necessary decline in the constant lurchings of the eternal see-saw of nature and life. And with every downward motion, there is sure to come an upward swing.

It is futile to resist change. It is self-defeating to refuse to turn a new page on the calendar. Like in the nature of seasons, there is beauty and truth in every age of human life, in every season of living. By moving with the seasons and by seeing a purpose in time, we can derive the fullest meaning of the moment. And if we "take care of the moments, the hours will take care of themselves," adding new and revitalized life to our years.

WE ACCEPT CHANGE AND SEE AUTUMN IN OUR LIVES

If you ever become despondent when you see fallen leaves of a past summer and the lengthening shadows of a nearing winter, stop and look, listen and observe.

There are sights on the horizon and voices in the air to brighten man's darkened soul. There is hidden mystery and splendor in ebbing colors and shades. There is a sweet melancholy in nature that proclaims change and prompts innovation and enthusiasm.

A green leaf on soggy ground is a sad sight, a gesture of resignation. But the tree beside it tells another tale. It is a solitary witness to an eternal and more reliable and recurrent cycle of life, of never fading promise. For every drying leaf, there is another leaf in the making, in expectancy of budding. Ice, snow and black skies can only shroud it in what seems to be an inevitable hibernation necessary to life.

There is a loveliness in nature, a grace that makes leaves blown in the wind as mystifying to our imagination as the freshly born blade that springs out of a deep freeze to burst into new life. There is an economy in nature, a brilliance of cleansing and dusting, pruning and revitalizing—a cosmic vacuum cleaner at work giving newness and freshness to weary leaf, branch, root and soil. And with it comes rest to teeming life and pause from dazzling heat and growth.

The sun is cutting corners today and is hiding in chilly air and gloomy clouds. But the sun's circle is reliably round and perfect. Beginning and end are merged; light and darkness are co-mingled into the perennial completeness of a globular whole.

Seasons provide us with a variety of beauty. And all elements in nature are fair. It is what we ascribe to them and the way we learn to live with them that makes the difference in what we see. There is a splendor even in the dark of night, a delicacy in slumber, a comely serenity in retreat. And the sensitive ear will listen to the voices of change and welcome them as the inscrutable rule of all life and all creation.

Beneath the fiery sun of a distant glow, you can still hear the chatters, the calls of birds in migratory flight. They are departing, but to return again; they are leaving, but to come back and rebuild their shattered nests, as soon as change one day not far off will usher in a warmer season and brighter days.

The wisdom of birds can be instructive. They have no time for sad lamentations. They mourn not last summer and a lost spring. An inner urgency of life impels them to embark upon their long journey of survival. They will die if they learn not to live with change, with the seasons, with transition. They linger not idly for devastating winds to pluck away their feathers and to chill their breath of life. They survive to sing another spring's song of life because they are too busy living and flying to surrender to winter gloom and doom. They cross mountains, rivers and lands and rise skyward so that the cold earth will not overcome them.

Everything in nature—even fall's deeper night—tells us of transition and movement, not of finality and end. A cold November day is only a partial summary of leaves and a certain stage of life. But by no means is it the signal of fatal descent and impending death.

We can enhance life with enthusiasm and beauty if we add the vision of faith and optimism to the sights of falling leaves and howling winds; if we summon the hope of confidence when black clouds seem to darken our horizon; if we escape sorrow by an upward flight, to rise again with the sun and to rebuild our battered nests with the dawning of a new spring in our life.

WE ACCEPT CHANGE AND SEE WINTER IN OUR LIVES

Winter is cold reality. It's a time of dismal rain, howling winds, drifting snow and frozen air. It is a time of deep sleep, pale lights and halted life, but not total retreat, not absolute retirement, not final decay.

Winter is a necessity of life and time, when the seed of life is secretly conceived. It is a season of expectant waiting, when wonder is hidden and sunlight is eclipsed. But deep down, sap is mounting, bud is swelling, roots are refueling. "The juice of life, buried, is quietly at work." It's not death in nature; it is rather diligent restoration to new life. And high above the precipitous overcast, the sun is still shining and moving toward a closer return in ever-widening circles.

True, it requires faith to perceive hidden mystery, when the eye can't see it. It takes fortitude to glimpse spring in mid-winter, when dead is the vegetable kingdom and desolate is the domain of life, and numb is the earth. But it's not clumsy death that rules the earth; it's pregnant life that is in waiting, in secret ministry. The eye doesn't behold it; it is a buried mystery. Dried up skeleton trees stand stiff like ghosts in solitary prayer. Songbird symphony seems such a long time in the past and spring is so far off. Yet, will it not come?

We know it will. We have faith—a feeling and experience of this certainty. It's only a question of time. There is sure to be rebirth, rejuvenation and rejoicing in the air. But meanwhile, we pause and take a deep, long breath and waste no time in waiting and in wooing a spring that isn't here yet.

We can crown the precious hour with warm delights, fireside enjoyments and intimate homemaking. The wintry, short-tempered sky is not inviting. But the "home comforts of a low roof, of undisturbed family living, of uninterrupted togetherness, of home-born happiness," are prospects to warm the heart and dispel the chill.

"There is . . . a time to cast stones and a time to gather stones." And what can be a better time to gather strength, to refuel, to relax from the outside tyrannies of scolding winds and cruel realities than at wintertime! In the warm stillness of the home and the heart, we may even come to discover a truth of life, that "into each life some rain must fall, some days must be dark and dreary."

But doesn't rain have a purpose and the dark an end? Would we really appreciate light if there were no darkness, warmth if there were no cold, spring if there were no winter?

Our human insight and vision give us the capacity of glimpsing the infinite glories of a future spring, with bright warming sun. However, our greater grandeur lies in our ability to transform immediate oppressive gloom into gleaming reality and hope. When there are shorter days, we can lengthen them with our own light; when there are bone-chilling nights, we can fire them with sparkling embers; when there is frozen air, we can create our own room atmosphere. We can transform a cold, desolate world into splendid and life-throbbing space.

The elements are here. The opportunities are at hand.

It is up to us to accept change as inevitable, and welcome it as a gift lavishing upon us a variety of new challenges, new possibilities and new horizons.

It takes no optimist to be cheerful and happy and peppy at springtime. Everything else is! How can one be less than exuberant in bright sunshine! But it takes a man, a real thinking and feeling man, to greet the gray winter morning with a smile and stay cheerful throughout the day; to feel the thawing smell of spring in the air, the inevitable change that will usher in a new spring, as sure as it thrust winter upon us.

For the faithful and the waiting, there is always this ever-abiding certainty: Through all the lifeless branches and the stark naked desolation of decay, we see, as could never better see, how the stars shine; how flickering lights sustain us in the promise of a new spring and life to come. The winter of life, as the life of winter, always comes to a happy ending.

WE ACCEPT CHANGE AND SEE SPRING IN OUR LIVES

Do you want to become a new person? Go outside, take a lesson from Mother Nature and you'll find her to be the grand teacher of all time.

You'll find that no matter what happens during the cold and lifeless winter days, spring is here again. Winter always passes when spring is in the air. The urgency of life's renewal is upon us. Sap is bursting into a new juice of life. Buried expectations of cold and dormant growth now begin to stir afresh, repeating the cycle of rejuvenation. When decay and decomposition are turned anew into bud, flower and leaf, grandeur and beauty, you know that death is not victor, that renewal and inner life's transformation is at the root of all things.

Spring tells us through color and green, through teeming life and the song of birds, that everything is possible—everything is miracle and nothing is so natural as miracle itself.

It is self-made and self-served; we have nothing to do with it. We can count the days, watch sunsets and sunrises, mark the calendar, till the soil, but this has nothing to do with the strengthening of the sun, the lengthening of days and the quickening of life's renewal—it's the wonder of wonders of life itself, reaching into the mystery of all beginnings.

Most of us will not admit it, but the real struggle is in the heart of man, not in the streets and in the marketplace. We want to know not only who we are but also what will become of us; we are yearning for immortality and are concerned over what might be the final end. And all our sophistication and genius is of no help to us. We still cannot duplicate leaf and life. We are still ignorant of the hidden secrets of life and the chilling mystery of death.

But when cold knowledge and understanding fail, warming faith and hope begin. In the ordered pattern of life and the universe—in spring's renewal—we find a logic that is ordained by the Power invisible and more inscrutable than the human mind can conceive; a truth more enduring than the brevity of life; "an understanding that reaches into meanings and symbols that demand nothing more than faith and hope, and need nothing else."

On a spring day it is easy to be hopeful, faithful and fanciful. If this season of awe and wonder can do such marvels with inanimate nature, if spring can transform the rotten juice of decayed life into renewed vitality and the dry bones of lifeless trees into new bloom, why cannot we similarly attain new powers and renewed life and the hope of immortality?

The message of spring is hope and confidence—hope everlasting, confidence to no end. Let us not neglect nor defer it when it comes. For what good is miracle and wonder if there is no eye to see it. Celebrate! Celebrate nature! Celebrate yourself by reaching out for that certainty—through faith and hope—that gives meaning to all life.

Spring summons rejoicing in discernment: to have eyes that see wonder, ears that hear sweet song, hearts that perceive faith and minds that conceive vision; to have strength and to know how to use it; to have love and to know how to give it.

WE ACCEPT CHANGE AND SEE SUMMER IN OUR LIVES

Summertime is fulfillment of promise. It is delivery after the long expectancy of rolling seasons. It's golden ripening to the brim of fullness—dream's reality, high life intensity of teeming and tingling growth. And the heart leaps joyfully and gratefully.

Growth is rather quiet. No tree brags about its gigantic size, its enormous leaf power, its natural beauty. No blade of grass demands gratitude for its industrious chlorophyll. No flower declares its glory, its grace, its distinctiveness of color and splendor. The giant breathing of nature is soundless, busying itself with the task of respiration, purification and beautification. And this silent harmony never dies because it's in the certainty of life that goes back to the source, the secret of its perpetual power. Nature doesn't proclaim its power. It is underscored by its quiet dignity and humility. The haughty tree that doesn't bend, breaks and dies. Real beauty is not luxuriant and expensive. The demands of flower and leaf are modest: sunshine above, water below, and fresh air around.

The soul of man expands in summer. The whole world takes on a new life of shimmering lights, of a deeper green, of a higher sky. Days are more rounded and expanded, compensating us for the shorter and grayer winter days. Nights are no longer enveloping and enshrouding with their wintry seal of dark mystery and abruptness. Night, when finally and quietly dimming, does not descend in a sudden roll of depressing black, but in the gentle and happy ending of a long and generous evening.

Summer takes no short cut to life. It absorbs life to the last drop of its potential. It makes up in industry and growth for the long sleep of a dormant winter. It soaks up warm sunshine as it takes in every drop of rain and dew. Summer lasts not forever, but while it lasts, it acts as if its dominion will always endure. And it does. Because it is always here to return. No matter how bitter the winter, with cruel and wailing winds, numbing frost and cold temper, it never succumbs to opposing forces in failing to spring to new life, to new spring, to new summer.

And if flower and tree could speak in human tongue, they might have turned to their natural inhabitant, thus saying: Man, learn from the ways of nature. Learn how to live from life itself, from elemental, unsophisticated pastoral life. It's open wide and yet so singularly self-rooted in itself; so deep and secretive in its silent brooding and yet so outgoing and co-mingling with the world; so alone and solitary in its own strength and growth and yet so harmoniously partaking of the whole of creation.

Go, then, man, to the source. Take a lesson of life from life itself. Welcome the new day as the birds greet the sun with the best song they know. Touch the dew of life, like the leaf that sparkles with the wet diamonds of a fresh early morning. Learn that quiet is not death, but the perpetual motion of a world of chlorophyll, of silent industry, of grass blades and tree leaves, catching their deep breath of bloom and growth.

We are closer to tree and bird than to machine and wheel. Ours is the rhythm of song and the pause of silence, not the endless clatter and din of motor and metal. There is nothing in living we can learn from the machine. There is much in nature that we can emulate.

Living, breathing, feeling requires openness. Live with the earth of your origins by intimately knowing it, by feeling its immense and growthful powers. Go out to the woodland and hear the message of life without words. Feel the open dimensions of everyday in this open and teeming season. Expand in its wide space, with its open generosity. And when you can hear the message of summer in the air, the intimations of the origins and the very source whence man and grass sprang from the generous hand of God, your own self and sensibilities will expand in the "quiet dignity of burgeoning green and spreading petal."

The gaiety of an active industry, automated by the mysterious hand of some unseen power, permeates all. Growth and fulfillment is joy; and in summertime you can't hide from it. You are drawn to it by that magical hand that made all beginnings. And you go to the source because you too have a beginning and an origin; because you want to be yourself for a change; because you need a change of scene to refresh yourself; because you know you must let yourself go.

So you join the seasonal exodus of vacationers and leave the din of city and town behind you. You go to the woodlands, to the seashore, to the mountains; you go searching, hunting, fishing.

What are you aiming at? What do you expect to find?

Yourself! Your simple unsophisticated and indigenous self. And you can find yourself and know your identity as well as your firm reality in this solemn hush of sprouting and marching green, in the scent of meadowland, in the lump of earthy freshness, in the enduring certainty of the source.

Here the enhancing language is life itself, eloquent and undeniable proof of rootage and fruition. Here you see the visible proof in the patient persistence of the "mighty oak," which "is just yesterday's little nut that held its ground." Here you learn the beauty of sound in the gleeful singing of birds and bees that never weary of song. Here you find a kinship with tree and leaf, and are humbled to acknowledge the simplicity of your human self, knowing that all your machines still cannot produce a living tree, a seed.

That's why you get away from it all: to search for yourself; to hunt yourself; to listen to yourself; to hear the poetry of trees; to see the visible workings of life at its source; to touch the dew of a new day; to feel refreshed, in tune with the universe and not shackled to the clatter of the machine.

In the retreat of mountain, ocean and hillside, you are brought back to your banished paradise for a reunion. And when you make your acquaintance with the tidal waves of ocean's ebb and flow and the stubborn persistence of hills and fields, you feel buttressed and stronger. You sense life's imperative within your bones and know that you are a living and feeling and knowing part of it, root and all. And as you don't question a bird's reason for singing, you start singing for no reason yourself. And as you don't challenge the strength of a tree's roots in adjusting to anchorage and growth, you feel like growing and adjusting yourself. Because life and laughter is upon you and vanished cares are behind you.

See it with flowers and leaf, is the order of the day. Summertime is not a time of philosophizing, not a time of dreaming, not a time of temporizing. It's reality in the fullness of delivery. Never mind the fleetingness of the flower, the brevity of the summer, the abruptness of growth. Live in the reality of a full summer day and feel no regret. Summertime is a time of doing: doing away with daily cares and irksome civilization and doing something with your simple living self to "see into the life of things."

There is a perpetual certainty and truth in leaf and flower that should remind us of our own eternally resurrecting powers. Today's life and growth draw their urgency and strength from winter's dead decay and buried expectations.

There is a perpetual certainty and truth in beauty to the eye that beholds it, to the ear that receives it and to the soul that perceives it—to all willing hearts. Summertime is all certainty, truth and miracle. It is easy to believe when you see; it is clear to understand when you marvel. It is all faith when you are awed. A reverence for the wonder of life and creation seizes you. You need no convincing. It is all documented in blades of grass, in color of flower, in song of birds. There is nothing unreal and fake about it. No tree, rose, violet or lily has ever made a promise to us to reappear on the universal scene and deck it with splendor. Yet they are always there on time, readily emerging in their industry of chlorophyll and beauty—as steady and as sure as sunrise follows sunset. They are voiceless as they are serene and so busy giving off fragrance and beauty that they have no time for quibbling and chaffing. Their span is too short to be wasted on murmuring and empty talk. Growth, wonder and glory are not the legacy of the smug and idolent.

In summertime, deep down in the primal elements, there lies not only beauty and truth and universal certainty and order, but also our own secret hope for perpetual growth, for fullness of maturity and the promise of our own everlasting presence in God's scheme of things. From all that we see in summertime foliage and infinite life, we know that miracle is all around us and with us (even if we call it nature). And seeing it all around us, we will come to believe that miracle is also within us and that perpetually restored beauty is the emblem of our own condition and the promise of our everlastingness.

11.

THE STAR CATCHER

Come, my friends,
'Tis not too late to seek a newer world.
To sail beyond the sunset, and the baths
Of all the western stars.

—Tennyson

MAN UNBOUND. WHEN THE WINGLESS EAGLE OF MAN finally landed on the moon, earthbound Adam became a new man. He was given a new birth and a new freedom, cutting his umbilical cord with mother earth and gaining a new identity. Call him what you may—magnificent bungler, strange intruder, dauntless explorer—he is above all affirmer and witness bearer. Being bored with his old world, he always seeks new worlds. In newness, he finds his own renewal and affirmation.

But this time, the measure of man's venture is the dimension of the stars themselves. His adventure now is wingless, airless, weightless (and in time may prove timeless) through the skies to other worlds in the universe.

This generation that was awed to the wonder of the newest testament—to the unprecedented sights of pillars of puffy fiery clouds sending man for the first time to another world—is stunned to dizzying stammering. What new eloquence is there for us to describe this new and liberated man in his newest dimensions, after breaking away from the shackles of his earthbound imprisonment? What art, what fiction, what myth is there that cannot, in the end, become man's precise science and firm reality?

We have watched from our living room TV sets that "one small step for man, one giant leap for mankind," but we cannot comprehend its immensity; we have seen our earthlings become moonmen but fail to grasp the ultimate infinity of their first footprints in the outer universe. It's revelation at its highest, wonder at its most wondrous, biblical at the most miraculous. And happy is the age, sublime its destiny, in having witnessed such aesthetic spiritual experiences of man the affirmer, man the dreamer, man the creator—ascending the heavens and mingling with the stars. We are, after all, not only God-like in our own little world but also God-free to roam the heavens like celestial creatures and creators.

In this new birth of man, in this new freedom of man, a new age has commenced: the Moon Age. And what William Blake envisioned in his time, in poetic mysticism and prophetic vision, we have come to observe today in scientific earthly reality: "To see a world in a grain of sand . . . Hold infinity in the palm of your hand And Eternity in an hour."

Scientists have turned to moondust with the same fascination of Blake's earlier ecstasy "to see a world in a grain of sand," to find traces of the birth of our solar system, to discover clues to the origin of this world and perhaps life itself. Geologists today possess the precious untouched dust of eons and treat it as if they were to "hold infinity in the palm of your hand . . . eternity in an hour." They seek to merge the mysteries of past billions of years with the knowledge of present science. Art has been matched with life, fiction with fact, myth with reality.

What remains now is to see the quality of our living come up to the colossal size of our dreaming. It has been said that when the two-legged creature became toolmaker, he ceased to be monkey and became man. But this is only partially true. For man can cease being monkey and still not be man. Man is man only when he believes he is man. Because for all his ingenious structures, enfolding himself in tons of metal, miles of wire, rivers of fuel and millions of pounds of thrust power, hurtling in heaven can be machine-man, robot-like creature, super technician, magnificent performer. It is only when he turns his art and his mind upon himself that he proves "little lower than the angels," and affirms his individual identity as well as his firm reality. Not in metal but in mental expansion will man prove his humanity and manhood.

Perhaps the new age of discovery into the new worlds of interplanetary exploration and into life itself may yet bring us new and undreamed of dimensions in the quality of our living here on earth. We may prove once again, as it was never proven before, that man's destiny lies in affirmation as much as in creation, in his awareness as much as in his velocity and movement. Perhaps a new identity of sublimity as well as humility will enter our consciousness to see our world as it really is from the view of another world: a tiny mote of loveliness, of velvet blue, of fiery brown, of trailing white clouds, precariously hanging on to a black infinity in time and in space.

New man can now take a new look at his old world— see it as it is and become eager to make it as it ought to be —and become so bored and so restless with it as to rise to this world's challenges as he is stirred to the challenge of new worlds, to begin the task of refashioning and recreating this lovely earth of his in his newer image of glory and ecstasy.

". . . ONE GIANT LEAP FOR MANKIND"

It is a power given to man to hurl his commands at nature and, by sheer strength of will and resolute determination, to alter the impossible. Thus it was in the far distant dawn of time when hairy-man crouched in the smoky firelight of his cave and began to dimly wonder about the outside world; and thus it will be to the end of man's time on this earth and other earths.

The biblical scene of Joshua standing in the field and ordering nature to accommodate him: "Sun, stand thou still upon Gibeon; and thou Moon, in the valley of Aijalon," is symbolic of man's audacious nature in defying the impossible, in challenging the impenetrable.

Why? Because the sheer exhilaration of exploration, venture and adventure are part of his curious character. And it is primarily this quality that sets him apart from the rest of the animal kingdom. For it, he sacrificed his pastoral calm and lost his innocence. Curiosity got the best of him when he reached out for that tantalizing apple in the garden and was condemned to death.

But he would rather lose his earthly paradise and his life than lose his capacity to gaze into the infinite distances of the stars; his lonely passion for ideas and ideals; his willingness to endure beyond measure for the climb of the ascent; his readiness to defy danger, disdain grief and sacrifice life itself for that which he considers larger than life, a new frontier: "One small step for man, one giant leap for mankind."

The most astonishing thing about this mammal, man, is not his technical skill as much as his distant vision. He is of nature, yet above nature; half animal, yet half God. He is contained in nature—a speck of dust in time and space—yet in comprehension he contains the universe.

In size he stands half way between the tiny microbe and the stars. But his vision encompasses the outer dimensions of galaxies. And what he cannot see, he believes he can envision; and what he believes and envisions, in the end proves real.

All that man conceives—fancy, dream, myth—must be, or else he wouldn't have dreamt it in the first place. This then is the inner truth of man: Maddening, unrealistically real and fantastic. Imagination is his trade, vision his obsession. He will let his foot dangle from an ungainly insect-like craft to set a shadow in another world in the cold solar system. Why? Because it's there!

It is this quality of the creator rather than of mere architect, of the fashioner of worlds rather than the toolmaker, of the dreamer rather than the manipulator, which sets man in a class all by himself, quite God-like in image.

And what is most admirable in man's voyages to the other and newer worlds is not the miracle of his machines and the wonder of his calculating precision, but the miracle within miracle: His spanning faith and long-range vision.

"What I admire in Columbus is not his having discovered a world," said A. Robert Jacques Turgot, "but his having gone to search for it on the faith of an opinion." We, too, must admire the Columbuses of our time (and all of us collectively are modern Columbuses) not for having discovered yet another world, but for our spiralling vision and daring thought in embarking upon an imaginary voyage leading to the stars—all of which began with the faith of an opinion.

What we must admire most is man's adventuresomeness

in opinions of faith and vision: To see and to know the moon, as it is in remarkable detail, even before he set foot on it; to see and to know the light years of a hundred thousand million stars of a galaxy within a hundred thousand million galaxies in the universe; to measure their astronomical distances and compositions, even while a tiny parasitic microbe can eat away at his frail mortal coil, averaging less than six feet in size. If this be the work of science, then science is workable faith.

It is this enigmatic something; this maddening outsized fantasy and wonder made so real by faith, hard work and the ecstasy of man's curious nature that makes him the romantic creature of the universe, in which all hope and glory lies.

THE UNIVERSAL DREAMER

Man, the incurable romantic, is the universal Dreamer. Dream is a power given to him, a power without which existence would become intolerable. It's his self-extension.

Horse power is mightier than human muscle, so man dreamt up steam power, electric power, combustible power, atomic and hydrogen power. The sparrow's wings can outsoar the upright walking mammal, so man invented a flying machine, jet propulsion, rocket thrust, human weightlessness. The eagle retina is keener in sight than the human eye, so man came up with magnifying lenses, the telescope, the microscope, X-ray, radar, high frequency radio sighting.

The Dreamer dreams up things and has the quality of extending himself infinitely, in earth's space, in ocean's space, in cell's space, in soul's space, in heaven's space. When he can't live under water he makes fins and scales out of some metal, some wire, and with some fuel navigates his depth-boring submarines. When he can't go up to the sun, he brings a form of sun-energy down upon his island earth, in the mushrooming shape of nuclear power. And now at last, he went up to heaven to catch the first and closest planet on his long and lonely path to the stars.

The Dreamer is Joseph of the ages, young in cosmic life, but bold in inner vision. Totally eccentric and audacious, he envisions the universe bowing to him: the sun, the stars, and the moon, the earth with all its treasures—all surrendering their secrets and some precious elements to him. He thinks himself central even among the stars. And even when he quotes his sciences and computations to prove his infinitesimal nothingness in the arch of the great heavens, in his heart of heart he believes in himself. He is more inclined to cite his human impulses and join Professor Stewart in silent consent, "we feel that we are greater than we know."

The Dreamer is not reduced to dying humility by the dwarfing infinity of the stars outside himself. Neither is he intimidated by menacing armies of infinitesimal microbes within himself. The first might easily destroy his soul, the second his body. But he is not distracted by the reality of things as seen by the eye and measured by the instrument. He must have an atomic soul that the soul itself cannot gauge. Can an eye look at itself, can a cell observe itself, can a soul weigh its own power?

There is no scale to weigh extended-vision, creative-spirit, the living soul. Size is a hollow concept, an illusion of unreality. Only the Dreamer with his dream is closest to reality, for he can grasp possibilities even before they are visible and create reality.

The Dreamer looks up. He first raised his eyes to the next hill, then to the next mountain, then to the next continent, then to the continents of another world. He can now watch the earthrise from another unearthly world by the glowing vision of his mind.

But the Dreamer also knows that for every depth of outer space, there must be an equal depth of inner space (a molecule of hydrogen, we are informed, vibrates more than 450 million times per second). And that the inner space of man—his inward self—is in need of mastery as much as outer space conquest is for the adventurist spirit.

There are the many spaces to be conquered on earth— the many wildernesses of man, the many gaps, the many desolate jungles of humanity. And as outer energy must be controlled against pollution, so must the inner energy of the Dreamer be mastered, lest a similar energy pollution that beclouds his outer world will also dim the light of his inner world, the soul. For man, the romantic, will not be happy with the beautification of physical nature only. He must also seek the beautification of his human nature.

". . . ON A TINY PLANET"

The Dreamer's future is uncertain, his past is haunting. He looks down into the ooze of his primeval staircase and finds his heart as primitive—if not more so—as in the days of Cain. This very same human race of master technicians that refined the art of ascent toward the stars also perfected the art of a descent toward hell's deepest hell—Auschwitz . . . the holocaust of super-technician's death . . . the ghastly gassing of more than a million children, of more than five million men and women . . . the crematoria . . . man's invention of the most technological and efficient hell . . . I had seen it written on the walls of a museum:

One Eon—Not so long ago, on a tiny planet of a minor star on the edge of a galaxy somewhere in space, certain molecules met in a sea of mud and life happened . . .

And ever since, the Dreamer is struggling to pull himself out of that primeval mud and mire of primitive life. And there are times when he occasionally succeeds, when he rises above himself to catch a star, a moon, a world. For intelligent man is more than a product of life that happens. His destiny is to be a producer of life in happiness.

Long ago we were told, and it's still true today: "He that is slow to anger is better than the mighty; and he that ruleth his spirit than he that taketh a city." Today, we may even be ready to conquer the planets of space, but our anger is not slow and our spirit is even less mastered. We are master technicians, but our soul is restless. We can make of heaven our earth, but can we make of our earth a heaven?

Human life today isn't becoming easier, in spite of prosperity and opportunity. We may have more but we enjoy less; we may be smarter, but not wiser; we may gain more knowledge, but less discernment. Why? Because we have too many distractions, too many contradictions, too many choices, too many opportunities—a fullness that keeps us jumping and empty, a variety that leaves us suspended, half-fulfilled.

Look at our pitiful contradictions, at our scandalous paradox. We are suspended between heaven and earth, between our ascent and descent. Up there, in the weightlessness of space, we are leaping into the cosmos and our thoughts sweep the heavens. But down here, the pressure cooker engulfs us and the ruthless race muddles us, and we are tearing ourselves apart and sinking back into the animal mire.

The astronauts in one Apollo spacecraft were one day puzzled by strange radio signals that were received by their communication network. They suddenly heard the song "Where Angels Fear to Tread." The source of the song creeping into their airless waves could not be revealed. But its theme was suggestive and most revealing, an appropriate theme for a glorious adventure. We are, after all, more angel than ape, because we can dream; we can sing and renew ourselves. In our renewal and in our spirit of adventure, in our daring and hoping, in the scope of our vision and in the range of our dreams, in our lonely passion for ideas and in our silent devotion to faith, we stand on earth with our ladder reaching into the higher heavens.

The Dreamer dreams and believes. We know God is; our thoughts and visions of Him prove it. (And as our mathematics of heaven have proved correct, so must our science of God be true.) But we also know that God is with us and favors us; our good earth with its living and hospitable conditions prove it. With a view from the moon and a vision of space, the real paradise in the black expanse of void is still our Mother Earth—an oasis of life, green, water, wind and color. To us the living, it is still the best of all possible worlds, if we learn to live in it together as friendly and cooperative co-pilots, bound together in a common voyage in the eternal ocean of time and space. And if the staircase of man inevitably stretches into infinite space toward a new heaven, the Dreamer can never forget that it is more important to have heaven come down to man than to have man go up to heaven.